EXPERIENTIAL RELIGION

EXPERIENTIAL RELIGION

Richard R. Niebuhr

HARPER & ROW, PUBLISHERS
New York, Evanston, San Francisco, London

1817

The author is thankful to the following persons and publishers for their permission to include excerpts from copyrighted matter:

Mr. Conrad Aiken for the line from *Senlin: A Biography* in *The Collected Works of Conrad Aiken.* Copyright © 1970 by Conrad Aiken. Published by Oxford University Press, New York.

Dr. Kathleen Coburn for excerpts from *Inquiring Spirit: A New Presentation of Coleridge from His Published and Unpublished Prose Writing.* Copyright © 1968 by Kathleen Coburn. Published by Pantheon Books, Inc. New York.

Dr. J. Glenn Gray for the passage from his book, *The Warriors: Reflections on Men in Battle.* Copyright © 1969, by J. Glenn Gray. Published by Harper & Row Publishers, New York.

Princeton University Press for entry 2398 from *The Notebooks of Samuel Taylor Coleridge,* edited by Kathleen Coburn, Bollingen Series L (copyright © 1961 by Princeton University Press), Vol. II, Text, 1804-1808.

Alfred A. Knopf, Inc., New York, for the entries from *Markings* by Dag Hammarskjöld. Copyright © 1964, by Alfred A. Knopf, Inc.

George Braziller, Inc—from *The Words* by Jean-Paul Sartre; reprinted with the permission of the publisher. Copyright © 1964 by George Braziller, Inc., New York.

FIRST EDITION

LIBRARY OF CONGRESS CATALOG CARD NUMBER: 70-163163

Designed by C. Linda Dingler

Contents

c.1

For

NANCY

From Ephesus to Cripple Creek

Acknowledgments

Johan Huizinga said, "I had to write now, or not at all. I wanted to write." In my case, my wanting to write would have been without result, had not a number of friends come to my help. First in my mind is Samuel H. Miller, late Dean of Harvard Divinity School, whose memory I cherish; Professor Herbert W. Richardson, St. Michael's College, University of Toronto, and Dr. George Rupp, Johnson College, Redlands University, who gave decisive encouragements; and Mrs. Ruth Kooman who helps in a hundred ways every day, year in and out, and types swiftly and accurately against unreasonable deadlines.

Some of this material, Chapters 2, 3, and 4, appeared in modified forms in lectures delivered in Cambridge University, at the invitation of the Faculty of Divinity in 1966, and in the Swander Lectures at Lancaster Theological Seminary in 1968, and also in single lectures at several other places. Chapter 4 in virtually its present form was published in the *Harvard Theological Review*, Vol. 62, No. 2, April 1969.

I am indebted to several persons and publishers for permission to quote. Their names appear on page iv.

Foreword

The subject of this book is faith—its experiential forms and contents—and the manifestations of God. But since I am less concerned with doctrinal and dogmatic definitions than with the welter of personal experience, I can as well say that the subject matter is the history of the present-day counterpart of that man Mr. Little-Faith, of whom Christian and Hopeful once talked rather charitably as they made their roundabout way toward the Celestial City.[1]

Reference to these three figures in *The Pilgrim's Progress* may suggest to the reader that I hope to emulate John Bunyan in what I offer here. That is so, in one sense—though it is as much Bunyan himself as his allegory I have in mind—for it is my aspiration to do one of the things that Bunyan accomplished, namely, to portray recognizable faith within our world. But that is the limit of my aspiration, if such an ambition may call itself limited.

Today ordinary faith impresses us in other ways than by its

1. The characteristics of Little-Faith as Bunyan presents him are these: he lives in the "town of Sincere"; he is prone to the assaults of three familiar enemies, Faint-Heart, Mistrust, and Guilt, whom he can neither fight nor run away from; yet he is stubborn and tenacious. His vulnerability to these three "rogues" puts him in company with Great-Grace, among Bunyan's other figures, and with King David and the apostle Peter, whom these three made to be "afraid of a sorry girl." (See *The Pilgrim's Progress, from this World to That which is to Come*, ed. J. B. Wharey and R. Sharrock, Oxford [1960], 125-132.) Little-Faith's descendant is like him in having to contend with irrepressible forlornness, indifference, and a consciousness of responsibility far exceeding his power.

greater or lesser quantity. Of course, Mr. Little-Faith's strife with doubt has its analogies in us, and something about doubt appears in what follows. But there are other equally familiar if not as clinically fascinating features of our experience of being in and out of faith. There is, for example, a man's exposedness to the overwhelming variety of humanity in our age, to the woes and sufferings and restlessness of his millions of contemporaries. It is an exposedness to which we have opened ourselves with our technology and from which we cannot retreat. Correspondingly, we may choose other fitting names for the present couterparts of Mr. Little-Faith. With varying frequency in these chapters I do use semiallegorical names. License for this practice comes not only from Bunyan but from the contemporary usage that speaks of *homo ludens* (man the player), *homo religiosus* (religious man), *homo faber* (man the maker), and *homo politicus* (political man). It is a convenient, shorthand way of referring to ourselves as men shaped by certain dominant traits of our daily experience. The names I play upon here are radial man and *homo Christianus*, the latter being, as I explain on page 9, a sociologically and psychologically defined version of Bunyan's Christian. Radial man, on the other hand, may be too much my own conceit to be useful for others. I have not, however, been able to put him out of my mind. Therefore, I offer the following explanation of how he came into it.

Radial man began emerging into definition as a symbolic figure in a fleeting allusion that Rudolf Bultmann made in his essay of 1941, "New Testament and Myth."[2] The man who listens to the radio, Bultmann said, cannot believe in miracles. The point of this reference was that a radio listener belongs to his generation. He is shaped by its scientific milieu and therefore is necessarily skeptical of the Bible. Although the skepticism to which Bultmann called attention is important enough, another aspect of the radio listener's demeanor impresses itself more and more

2. See *Kerygma and Myth*, trans. H. Bartsch & R. H. Fuller, New York (Harper Torchbook, 1961), p. 5. But the British word wireless, in the English translation, does not suggest the association of ideas that Bultmann's *Radioapparat* called up.

deeply on the imagination. This aspect appears in the image of a man seated and somewhat bent, in an attitude of habitual, even involuntary attentiveness to the loudspeaker broadcasting messages of tidal waves, ambushes, coups d'état, and cholera epidemics. The strong suggestion is that this figure is passive. Since the radio is an extension of the ear, the radio listener occupies the position of a target into which impulses of energy penetrate from the whole globe and its environment. As a listener he has so extended the range of his awareness that he is disturbed by a far greater proportion of the sound and energy in his world than ever drummed upon the ears of any of his predecessors. Of course, many other instruments illustrate this taut and fatiguing watchfulness: the radio telescope, radar, U-2 aircraft, scanning satellites, and so forth. But the familiar word radio symbolizes the situation of the watcher better than any other word or image can. For radio, as dictionaries tell us, derives from radius, meaning ray and, by association, wave and packet: of light, of sound, of electricity, of atomic energy. The growing list of compound terms in which it appears suggests the extent to which the individual lives in a radial world, a world that bombards him with packets of force.

The quanta or radiations impinging on him are in part patterned and communicative waves of energy: sentences and expressions, harmonies, images, color arrangements, and so forth; and in part simple or chaotic energy, though the difference between the orderly and the merely accidental is increasingly problematical. But what is clear is that the radio listener lives in a radial world of energy, and the device itself is but one of the instruments that are transforming him into, and reminding him that he is, a being for whom immediate reality is power: power driving and moving him, distracting and destroying him, healing and shaping him. He is a radial man in a radial world.

Yet it is misleading to stress too much the apparent passivity of this person. For one thing, the responsibility belongs to him and his kind for having expanded the human senses. The consequences men bear today are the consequences of an action. More important is the fact that listeners and watchers do not merely absorb. Each responds to the energy impinging on him by cultivating patterns of conduct and belief. Bultmann, for example, understood the listener chiefly as a man subscribing to particular laws of physics. By his very action of listening, the listener shows that he believes that energy behaves in certain circumscribed ways, so that his skepticism of the Bible is but a negative consequence of his positive response to his environment. But it seems likely that this man's doubt is more complex and is not merely the product of his scientific tenets. He is not that logical or consistent a man. Like his fellows, he is quite capable of holding in his mind more than one system of beliefs, and if he were sufficiently interested he could entertain both a confidence in the orderliness of energy that enables him to operate a radio and a hope in the resurrection of all men. Doubt is as much a product of the listener's new measure of humanity as it is of his scientific ideology. His doubting grows also from his being asked to take part in too much. Witness the way in which many men today shink from the thought of immortality.

If we understand the listener's doubting not as simply lack of belief but as a concomitant of a way of responding to his radial world of power, the more fundamental issue he poses is the issue of the method or style he employs in his assimilation of power. The method of his reacting may be any one of many, but in any case neither the radio nor the laws of energy it represents provide a method for the appropriation of power. To commend itself a method must have a moral and religious authority. It is not only consistent but conceivable that the listener follow a Christian method in the world of power, a method of suffering the impingement of power which styles itself on Jesus of Nazareth. Indeed, insofar as Christianity originated in the human necessity of suffering, we may fairly say that the listener symbolizes the modern human situation Christianly as well as scientifically understood. It should be appropriate, therefore, to speak of radial man as symbolizing the universal destiny of suffering and the generic need of finding a way or method.

chapter 1
Geneses

I. New Earth—New Man

Not only do times and men change, as we expect, but so does our relation to the earth. The contrast between Theseus' worship of earth divinities and our grandfathers' restless eagerness toward this globe as a western territory awaiting its pioneers suggests the measure of this change. But today even the frontiersman is gone, gone from the land and going from our dreams. For we have placed ourselves in a new station in the earth, one for which we have no useful analogy except the most familiar and least understood of all, the connection between the mind and the body. We have married ourselves to our physical environment, and we exercise a control—a most tactful control—that can be compared only to the limited and mysterious authority of the mind over eyes and ears, heart and lungs, and our body chemistry. This intimacy carries with itself many penalties, of course, for just as each of us suffers mentally in bodily disease, so earthborn catastrophes bring on us collectively a more personal pain than men experienced when they endured earth's space as a temporary prison and sun's time as an affliction. In any case, the earth is not our mother. It is not the scene of our pilgrimage or probation, nor is it the theater of our adventures. It is now a strange thing, both organism and tool, supplying us life while at the same time giving us the means of altering our life's nature. The body for whose health and soundness the sound mind must now care is no less than the water, the land, and the air in which we live.

We are now feeling the first pains of the labor and self-denial to be exacted of us by this new stage of human self-determination: the necessities of managing the balance between animal, plant, and insect; of repurifying the atmosphere; of desalting sea waters; and of pondering the span of life to which a generation is entitled. Out of necessity, the human spirit has become a productive spirit on a hitherto unknown scale, and though this spirit is not precisely the absolute creating spirit, it is surely an architective spirit, shaping the matter of life. If any of us still picture ourselves in the images of Genesis, we realize that men have assumed a dominion of which the Priestly liturgists had no inkling. Or if we conceive ourselves on the hypothesis of evolution, then we perceive that we have appropriated the prerogative of Darwin's impersonal principle of natural selection and that henceforth the direction of our growth depends largely on what we shall deem to be natural or right or good for mankind. Therefore, one does not need to turn back to metaphysics to affirm what daily experience is teaching us, that the spirit in human nature is a shaping spirit, molding the tissues of life. Nor does one need to philosophize on the priority of existence over essence in order to believe that in shaping the structure of life man is making himself.

What the last and full outcome of this epoch may be none but a prophet could tell us. And such a prophet would need to know not only what powers we are acquiring but also what faith informs the power-ful.

But if we examine that part of mankind nearest us, which struggles wth its hope of redemption and fear of annihilation in this body, one great spiritual change in the human condition strikes us in particular. It is a concomitant of the new engagement between man and earth. We see, stating this feature in the most hyperbolic form, that the individual is the race. We should say more accurately that the individual is his generation. Generosity has become the fate of every man. Such a description of the individual's relation to his society does not depend on any mystical meaning of our words.[1] It simply states one result of our shaping art. With our communications technology we have extended our senses and our sensibilities in making the scope of our eyes and ears coterminous with the inhabited earth and its solar environment. There is no physical horizon over which the enemy can vanish. Without physical horizons no social or psychological distances remain to give credibility to the Psalmist's assurance: "A thousand shall fall at thy side, and ten thousand at thy right hand; but it shall not come nigh thee." Our electronic global nervous system relentlessly transmits the anger, fears, and hopes of every emerging nation and pent-up ghetto to the sleepless mind of the radio listener.[2] Even friendly beings, nations with common traditions, cannot disengage themselves for a time and shut off their lives from the anxious interest of their allies, not to speak of the orbital watchfulness of their enemies. The common human passions[3] and occasions for human sympathy pass long the earth's channels of intersubjectivity with speed and ease. Such unre-

1. Once the matter of the relation of the individual to his kind or species was a theological and philosophical issue. Now it belongs to sociology and psychology. But the moral terms in which individual and generic identity pose a problem for us remain constant. In what sort of identity is our responsibility for our kind rooted? We have more reason than ever to weigh Kierkegaard's thesis that "the individual is himself and the race. This is man's perfection . . . . Every individual is essentially interested in the history of all indviduals . . . . Perfection in oneself means therefore the perfect participation in the whole." (See *The Concept of Dread,* trans. Walter Lowrie, Princeton [1946], 26.) Jonathan Edwards also wrote of Adam and his descendants as "one complex person, one moral whole." (See *Original Sin, The Works of Jonathan Edwards,* vol. 3, ed. Clyde Holbrook, New Haven [1970], 391.)
2. See the Foreword, p. xii.
3. The word passion here and throughout bears its classical philosophical sense, meaning the state of mind resulting from *action upon* human being. *Emotion* has a much greater currency in modern usage than *passion,* but for that reason, no doubt, is too flexible and vague. See *Emotion: A Comprehensive Phenomenology of Theories and their Meanings for Therapy,*

mitting and extensive emotional sharing as this has multiplied by a ratio not yet calculated the susceptibility of the individual to emotional infection by his generation.[4] He lies pathetically enmeshed in the network of "constant contact news" and has no hour of the day, no sabbath rest, when he is not made to be a sharer in the abrading or engulfing sensations of other men.

Since we have so enlarged our capacity for simultaneity of experience, no longer needing time to overcome space, we live together on a new scale of inclusiveness and intensity. We live together the sharpness of the moment of assassination in Dallas, Burundi, and Tokyo, in Memphis, Saigon, and Los Angeles, of civil strife and killing in Orangeburg and Kent. Such modification of our sense is a radical alteration of our nature. A century ago, those who were philosophically inclined found it still necessary to use Plato's doctrine of universals to indicate how one man could be a vicar for others, Adam for his posterity, Christ for his brothers. But now no member of the civilized world has a choice but to be one who stands sensibly and morally in the places of others, even though he may lack strength for this role and succumb to spiritual destruction in it. It is no wonder that some persons try to deaden their sensibilities and insulate themselves in somnambulistic solitude. Chemical ecstacy or routine existence in the crowd, where the individual is simply "one" who does what "one does" and belongs to that anonymous society called "they," offers the blessedness of a sleeping life in which he is deaf to his nerve ends. In full consciousness the person who is vicar for his generation must bear the weight of an almost intolerable fellow-feeling.

---

by James Hillman, London (1962). The descriptions of passion by Thomas Hobbes in *Leviathan,* by Spinoza in his *Ethics,* and by Jonathan Edwards in his *Treatise Concerning Religious Affections* are still instructive. See below, chap. 2 for a fuller discussion of passion in relation to affection and mood.

4. Max Scheler distinguishes "emotional infection" from "fellow feeling" as an involuntary state that is uninformed by conscious knowledge of the dread or joy, etc., in the other person or persons. It is emotion inspired by kinship or some other association but unaccompanied by reflection. See *The Nature of Sympathy,* trans. P. Heath and W. Stark, New Haven (1954), 14 ff.

Here then is a partial view of the man of our new man-earth relation. He is a being on whom a vast field of encompassing physical, psychological, and moral powers converge, arousing and dampening his passions, modulating his affections. In a radial world he is a target, a victim, a vicar. Sympathy has become his lot, the vicar's responsibility his dread. Susceptibility to emotional infection and a drift toward anonymity have become common marks of his spiritual life.

Morbidity, however, is usually more striking to the eye than the symptoms of health, and it is unjust to this man not to note the features of his comportment that are less lurid but more significant. One especially stands out. This man does not face backward. Nostalgia clings, but he lives forward. He cannot affect the aristocratic mental and spiritual habits of the nineteenth century with its contempt of the masses. He does not seek to be a hero: Nietzsche's superman or Kierkegaard's solitary exister or Schweitzer's reverencer of all life. He takes his place, rather, in the ranks of the growing millions who must be ever more deeply disturbed and displaced in their inner lives by the pressures of others upon them. Unless he chooses to stupefy himself, he has no defenses except the homely virtues of courage, wisdom, justness, and temperance, leavened perhaps by a little faith, hope, and love. Nothing human is alien to him. But he does not make this his boast. It is only a fact he accepts.

II. Secular and Many

The ramifications that grow from this new reality are broad enough to overshadow the whole of the human scene and steep it in an unfamiliar light. In this light, human personality as it individuates and clothes the life of the race appears differently than it did before. Two other features of our present comportment tell of the change, features that are but further aspects of our destiny to be vicars of our generation. The first is the so-called secularity of man in this radial world. The second is his inner manyness. They are so intimately related that, while we should distinguish them, we can describe them only together.

Secular is a much used and debated word. However, for our purpose of understanding humankind in its new relation to the great earth-body each man shares with all, we do not join in argument. It is sufficient to note and acknowledge the differing meanings of secular, which vary according to the differing interests that move us to interpret what has happened and what is happening to us. When, for example, our interest lies principally in explaining how the past was a cause of the present, then we cannot overlook the dramatic decline, from the sixteenth century to the twentieth century, of the Christian church as a chief agent of universal culture and shaping influence upon the race and the seemingly inexorable ascent of commerce and industry to that standing. In our social history, therefore, secular names the forms and spheres of life that acquire their character through their opposition to the sacred. Looking back, we may rightly say that each generation between Luther and Freud was more secular, viz., less profoundly touched by religious institutions, than the foregoing. That, then, is the historical meaning of secular: not the meaning secular bore in former times but the meaning it carries in historical science.[5]

On the other hand, we in the present experience the present effects of past causes, not the past causes themselves. Accordingly, our experience owes much to the process of secularization of the past. But the secularity we experience is different—different enough in degree as to be different in kind. For the distinctive element in our lives is not the ascendancy of one institution over another, the greater authority of banks and the diminished authority of churches. It is, instead, the diminished authority of all forms, spheres, and institutions of our life together that differentiates our age. The consequences for our life in its customary forms, in

5. The old ecclesiastical distinction between the secular and the religious priest carries, perhaps, the meaning closest to our experience of secularity, for the conversation and conduct of the secular priest is that of his ordinary neighbors—even though he has a specialized vocation—and not that of a separated community.

family, school, and profession, as well as in church, are far-reaching and have touched us all. No longer is it the past embodied preeminently in a family or profession that endows a man with his personality. Rather, it is the whole age, laying upon him a more difficult obligation to play his part in the building up of a new common good.

That man is genuinely secular whose spiritual and mental milieu is the entire age in which we find him. For he does not remain a citizen of the place either of his physical or of his spiritual birth, be it a prairie town, the executive offices of an industrial dynasty, the headquarters of a political party, or a battlefield. His mind comes to belong to the times rather than to a place or community. His ordinary ways of thinking, his association of ideas, turns of speech, and aspirations symbolize more the experience of the whole generation with which he is incorporated in this earth than the customs of a site or settlement or house. The evidences of this trait of our times are plentiful, ranging from dress and speech to the most deep-buried images that govern human perception. In all of these moments of our lives the differences between classes and regions are growing ever less than the differences between generations.

We meet the secular businessman or politician as often as the secular Jew or Christian. Our secularity then is not the opposite of religiousness.[6] It is much more, and it arouses in the individual an unfamiliar awareness: he is fated to act a role in the economy of the whole age. Vicarious experience is the nucleus of this awareness; secularity of this new order is its first effect.

We recognize that in all likelihood we could not imagine such an awareness, let alone taste its reality, were it not for the scope and stress of the experience we have technologically augmented.

6. Mircea Eliade's striking portrayal of archaic religion surely illuminates our lives, but it is difficult to transpose the sacred-profane dyad into the present. No doubt we too celebrate sacred rites and mark off sacred from profane time in popular and civil as well as in churchly religion. But such observation of the sacred does not appear to belong to the essential structure of our experience. Professor Eliade's claims in fact seem moderate on this score. See *The Sacred and the Profane*, trans. W. R. Trask, New York (Harper Torchbook, 1961).

But still this awareness is the work of more than just one cause. The moral effects of our democratic creed and practice also increased it, and the ethos of our American free enterprise has fed it. The partly realized idea of democracy has contributed, because its professed intention is to make every individual a joint stock owner in the times, as it were. Republican convictions and laissez-faire practices have created for the individual a presumptive world in which he does not owe fief to any overlord but only the fidelity of his word to his fellows. Distinctions of person have disappeared, at least from our principles, for our fathers abandoned the vertically ordered society to bring up their children as citizens living on a single, illimitable plane. The old divisions to which Christendom clung so long have lost their authority: the divisions between grace and nature, church and world, elect and reprobate. Our political and economic ways have devalued these marks of different worth and fostered in us the disposition to accept the equal authority of all men. Political and social democracy have in turn drawn upon and encouraged a democracy of experience, in which the testimony of experience carries its own authority, commanding respect according to its greater or lesser authenticity and requiring neither metaphysical nor political sanction.[7]

Membership in this secular age can be costly and is so by necessity for the individual who sincerely seeks to act out a defined creed. Upon the Christian and Christianized it inflicts a

7. The late Professor Perry Miller interpreted the Great Awakening as a development in which democracy settled more firmly in America. The premium which revival preaching and doctrine placed on immediate, personal experience of grace tended to shift religious authority from the appointed and specially educated clergy to the laity and so to the common man. See *Errand into the Wilderness,* Cambridge (1956), chap. 6. This particular instance of the translation of authority into the domain of individual experience belongs to the wider movement of social history in Europe and America, including as dissimilar persons as practitioners of spiritual exercises and Puritan preachers and theologians, the British empirical philosophers of the seventeenth and eighteenth centuries, and the twentieth-century psychoanalytical school, all of whom developed methods for the analysis of the individual's experience as the key to health and truth. The democracy of experience has been extending itself gradually for centuries along many diverse lines.

threefold suffering of inner division.[8] First of all, by his profession, this individual in consenting to his religious duty cultvates his ability to be a vicar, to identify himself with his neighbor, with whatever stranger is near to him. Second, by having in himself the mind of democracy with its egalitarianism of authority he is obliged to value the experiences of others. And, finally, by virtue of his inherence in the electrified earth he stands in the place of many others, whom he neither knows nor has chosen, sharing in their passions and their needs.

The price of this multiple extension of his sympathy and sensibility is that he must and cannot help but take what others give him in their testimony as having a truth for him. There is no need to attribute to this secularized man a fresh resolve to believe, in each instance that he meets another's testimony. Rather, this attitude toward others is simply basic to his spirit and mental conduct. No communion of saints can protect the individual from the doubting of his fellows or from their other-mindedness. The testimony of doubt, of other-mindedness, and of indifference, in fact, now claims his attention as insistently and rightfully as did in former times the stories of assurance with which the saints comforted and strengthened one another. What has happened is

8. I believe it is legitimate for the purpose at hand to gather together the self-consciously Christian and the men who are Christian only by virtue of their cultural inheritance. However many differences we may perceive between them, we discern also a shared character or nature, for which it is convenient to adopt the name *homo Christianus*. In his sporadic or disciplined self-examination and meditation on the world and God, the individual belonging to this most inclusive class of western men invokes the name of Jesus. Jesus of Nazareth is the Christ he has upon his conscience, not perhaps in the narrow sense that he feels himself personally implicated because an innocent Messiah suffered and was crucified in the reign of Tiberias, but in the broader sense that he cannot think of himself without imagining this Christ to be one of those who are looking at him. Jesus Christ, in however clear or shadowy a form, has become an indelible face in the "generalized other" that reflects him back upon himself and shapes and informs his self-consciousness. In this sense, *homo Christianus* is the man who sometimes intentionally and often only routinely "follows" a Christian way, follows after Jesus of Nazareth. *Mutatus mutandi,* there are other kinds of religious men who are Messiah—or Christ followers—in our world: Jews, the older brothers of Christians, and Marxists, the younger brothers. For messiah may mean an anointed people, or person, or time.

that *homo Christianus*—both the professing and the acculturated Christian—has become a man distracted in the heterogeneity of his age, polarized between the witness of Jewish and Christian martyrs and the testimony of "negative" martyrs. He sees in un-faith an experience, a state of mind, as much to be scrutinized and inwardly tested as the heartfelt convictions of the saints.[9] The bearer of this expanded and intensified awareness cannot arbitrarily exclude the one for the other. To do so would be to vio-late the spirit and the code of the society that has endowed him with personality. But since of his own will and nature he may exclude no one, this man must welcome into himself—at least for a time—all who speak to him in a voice carrying the authenti-city of experience. As a vicar, he is condemned to become in-wardly many.

III. Doubting

The felt obligation to share other men's doubting is one com-mon experience of inward manyness characterizing this radial world. There are varieties of doubt, to be sure, and not all of them exercise what is so nearly a moral claim. That claim belongs to the doubting associated above all with religion and faith. But again not all religious faith shows affinity for doubt. It is the religion attuned to the new earth-man relation that ex-hibits it principally.

In the eleventh and thirteenth centuries, doubt and faith argued

9. Theologians have customarily met the greatest difficulty in treating the "absence" of Christian religion and faith as the effect of some cause or state of affairs, which insofar as it is a cause must be something. Many have regarded the absence of Christianity as an instance of "nonbeing," as a deficiency of reality, in a scheme of being symmetrically suspended from the Logos of God which is one with Jesus of Nazareth. The history of theology from Friedrich Schleiermacher to Karl Barth illustrates the problem. But that judgement does not correspond to the experiential world in which *homo Christianus* lives today, where an alien state of mind manifests the real rather than a measure of unreality. But not only does this theological judgment fail today, it does not correspond to the world that the Gospels describe either.

with each other, and faith made its way from earth to heaven on the ladder of dialectic with the Fool. Doubt was the Fool who said in his heart there is no God. Doubt was Boso who had no reasons, while faith in the persona of the theologian set forth the reasons of Reason itself, which when once manifested irresistibly elicited assent and belief from the clearheaded.[10]

Now another kind of doubting presents itself. It is something else than a lack of reasons for believing. It is not spiritless and docile. This newer doubt arises within our consciousness on the occasion of our encounters with alien interests and with the indifference of other men toward our own spiritual vision. Such doubt, although it has recognizable precursors in Pascal and the sixteenth-century reformers, shows the distinctive mark of our secular and democratic age: it emerges in the believer from the obligation he willingly accepts to engage with that which is strange, inimical, or indifferent to his believing.

The believer brings this doubting upon himself. Like Christian in Bunyan's allegory, *Pilgrim's Progress*, he must traverse the vicinity of Doubting Castle, for it is part of the geography of his own soul. This "vicinity" is nothing else than the presence in his mind of the whole saeculum with its great numbers that show an unlimited range of other sensibilities. In such a field of countless and diverse human beings as this, the multiplicity and variety of beliefs, dispositions, and attitudes embodied in endlessly differing personalities thrust the individual back on himself, so that he is struck with the immensity of the galaxy of human creeds surrounding him and the insignificance of his own hopes and doctrine.[11] Amazement drowns his former certainty: "This great

10. See Anselm of Canterbury's two treatises on which scholastic philosophy and theology and much modern thought rest: *Proslogion* and *Cur Deus Homo*.
11. In our nostalgia Bunyan's world appears as one of great simplicity. But he gives an account, in which the elements are timeless, of the invasion of doubt through the perception of the endless variety of mankind. "The tempter would also much assault me with this: How can you tell but that the Turks had as good Scriptures to prove their *Mahomet* the Saviour, as we have to prove our *Jesus* is; and could I think that so many ten thousands in so many Countreys and Kingdoms, should be without the knowledge of the

world of life in no relation to my own action . . . !"[12] Such astonishment is further reinforced by the moral sense of kinship binding him to these other beings despite their otherness. For though a man and all of his ways be foreign and even inimical to him, the Christ follower must nevertheless treat him as a true representative of being, as an end in himself, according to the imperative of democratic experience.

So it comes about that *homo Christianus* projects his imagination, tries to interpret his strange neighbor—and disastrously succeeds in discovering himself in the other. We do not need to suppose that any elaborate art of interpretation is put to work in this conversion to double-mindedness and uncertainty. It may just as well be the spontaneous transaction of a moment. By a word or gesture expressing his indifference the stranger rifts *homo Christianus* and discloses to him other personas within, waiting to be born.[13] At a public gathering—a dinner—while one member is saying the grace, another notices that Lord X, a famous and courageous moralist and atheist, does not bow his head but looks about with an expression of amusement; and that proud head calls to him, "You too would be such as I."

Doubt, especially self-doubting, is a spiritual mark of this age.[14] Some men have found satisfaction in boasting of it as their peculiar spiritual affliction. Such satisfaction, however, can be only

---

right way to Heaven (if there be indeed a Heaven) and that we onely, who live but in a corner of the Earth, should alone be blessed therewith? Everyone doth think his own Religion rightest, both *Jews,* and *Pagans;* and how if all our Faith, and Christ, and Scriptures, should be but a think-so too?" *Grace Abounding to the Chief of Sinners,* ed. Roger Sharrock, Oxford (1962), par. 97.

12. The exclamation is Willian James's, in *The Thought and Character of William James,* ed. R. B. Perry (Briefer Version), New York (1954), 224.

13. Tolstoy tells of such a conversion from belief to indifference through a casual word in *My Confession,* which William James includes among his examples in *The Varieties of Religious Experience,* New York (The Modern Library), 174 ff., n.

14. Doubting as self-doubt "caught" from the indifference and differentness of other men is only one form of doubt, and it should not be confused with other important forms, such as heuristic doubt, which Michael Polanyi describes and evaluates so well in *Personal Knowledge, Towards a Post-Critical Philosophy,* Chicago (1958), 276 ff.

short lived, for doubting is not limited to any elite. Furthermore, no surgery can exscind this condition nor any medicine of certainty cure it. Such pervasive doubting can be "overcome" only by suppressing it in moral sleep. But the man we have been describing cannot annul his contract with the society that has endowed him with his personality. To destroy the symptoms of doubting in this manner would be to destroy one's own moral identity.

The recognition of the futility of efforts to erase doubting from the present human condition has led some observers of our scene to believe that doubt and its kindred states of despair and dread are endemic rather than epidemic to humankind. The late Paul Tillich, foremost among them, developed an ontology of doubting man in order to reinterpret this traditional symptom of spiritual pathology as a manifestation of the power of being. In skepticism, accordingly, Tillich saw the mark of the finitude of human reason; and he dissected the doubter in his doubting until the act appeared as a moment of self-affirmation: a collision with the limits of the power of understanding that shocks the doubter into a new awareness of the "thereness" of his own being.[15] Doubting appears, in the view Tillich invites us to share with him, as a spiritual act in which the creature asserts its "facticity." *Dubito ergo sum.*

Whether we require or find truly useful an ontology of doubt may be debatable (although error and uncertainty, as much as any other features of our life, beg for explanation). But clearly we cannot attribute all doubting to the limitedness of our understanding or to the deficiency of our being, when it is the presence of other men in ourselves, through our imagination and sympathy, that gives birth to so much of our doubting. Curiously, or perversely, we are enriched by such uncertainty. Therefore, doubting is not simply a sign of weakness. It is, rather, one of the threads in the ever more complex web binding the individual into his generation. The prevalence of doubting attests the pervasiveness

15. See *Biblical Religion and the Search for Ultimate Reality,* Chicago (1955) and *The Dynamics of Faith,* New York (1957).

with which the saeculum is present in the individual. Never has
the individual been so much a conscious part of his age. Seldom
has he felt himself so compelled to join its attacks on his own
security.

Doubt does not exhaust the personality of man in this age,
nor is it even the most typical of our states of mind. What the
prevalence of such doubting does signify is the penetration of
the saeculum into all the recesses of the individual's soul. Doubting is the colored fluid that enables us to see the capillary attraction in our lives for the moods surrounding us. Intensive scrutiny
would reveal many other elements of the age working in us as well.

IV. Inventing

Experience of this order disrupts life in enclaves. Whether
it is the cause or the effect of the erosion of the old nuclear
communities of our society is obscure. But clearly men and women
today move on planes vaster than the precincts of any single institution or class. Neither the family nor the church nor the preserver
of culture, the school, establishes the pattern of the individual's
conduct or defines the horizon of his world. Even the shaping
role of the people or nation is diminishing.

Nevertheless, our awareness that our life is life in an age rather
than in a locality does not make us wholly forget the ancient
forms of life together. Family, school, church, university, and
nation live on in us and we in them, and much of human strength
and excellence still depends on the effective presence of these
forms. But the position of the individual in them has changed.
He has always been the necessary link in the continuity of institutions and the indispensable means for the preservation of
humankind. Today, however, he is not only shaped, as an infant,
in these social and generic forms; but, as an adult, he in turn
becomes their manager, a demiurgos with power to mold the
nexus from which he issued. In him the forms of life, no matter
how old or stylized they may be, become nascent and plastic,
awaiting his determinations.

This position of privilege and power is one that we do not customarily acknowledge as belonging to our contemporaries. It is easy and tempting to regard humanity as a lump rather than as a moral kind of being. In our disaffection toward the grey necessities of our time, it is even fashionable to view human nature almost wholly under the aspect of modernity we call mass culture, to perceive men as instances of *das Man*, the anonymous, "average," and empty neuter that rides in public transportation, reads the newspaper, and otherwise hides in the habits of "they" and "one."[16] But we should not permit this philosophy with its nineteenth-century aristocratism to blind us to the human realities of this age. For real and critical power accrues to the individual dwelling on the limitless planes of the present. The tides of shared experience encourage him to move, indeed they sweep him from his birthplace. They inexorably require of him choices: whether, where, and how to plant, to build, and to shape life anew. The destiny of secularity makes new beginnings an indefeasible responsibility.

Some welcome the flood of secularity as a purging deluge, expecting to behold a clean new country appear from beneath its waters, with all traces of old ways erased. Others lament the expunging of tradition. However, the break between the old and the new as most of us experience it is neither so total, so entirely full of promise, nor so darkly ominous as our different oracles like to say. As it befalls us, this breaking of the new day effects in us various and even contradictory moments of awareness. It comes upon us wearing the appearance of inexplicable necessity, or as the inevitable consequence of our own earlier actions, or as the challenge calling out our free response. What can, perhaps, be said of this ambiguous experience is that in fact it constitutes both an arduous transformation which is being wrought upon us and a transformation for which we must assume responsibility. It carries us deeper both into our fate and into our freedom. It creates at least a dual consciousness in us.

With this dual consciousness comes a deep uneasiness, whose

16. See Martin Heidegger, *Sein und Zeit*, Tübingen (7th ed., 1953), sec. 27.

depth is a measure of the changes overcoming us. Perhaps the most apt analogy for this pervasive feeling of *dis*ease is the moral and psychological position in which a man elected to public office first puts and then finds himself. The politician is the secular man drawn in strong lines. The congressman, for example, seeking to represent a district, when elected must represent the several towns of the district, and therefore he stands in a posture of discomfort, belonging to all and not belonging wholly to any of the centers of his constituency, indeed, discovering that in order to represent his electorate he must also represent the larger whole of which his district is but a part.[17] Like the elected representative, the citizen of the present age has a vocation he cannot shun to define for himself the relations between the different spheres of interest and power that inhere in his own being. Specifically, he has to map anew the changing shapes of the religious and the

17. The man newly elected to office begins as one who thinks and speaks in the idiom of his ward, his precinct, or whatever may be the constituency he has first chosen. But in the exercising of his office he becomes the target of other equally genuine, undeniably human aspirations and fears, modes of thinking and acting that sweep in upon him from a far broader range. His survival in office depends on his ability to sustain the resulting conflict in himself; to alter and accomodate his two worlds to each other, where possible; and to live a divided life, where accommodation is not possible. The politician becomes a field in which competing passions and other human forces clash. As the representative of at least two different worlds, he cannot belong wholly to either. When, in the legislative chamber on Capitol Hill or in the House of Parliament, he casts his vote, he declares himself—for the time being— a member of the precinct or of the city, of the district or of the nation, of the nation or of the earth. He gives shape in himself to one of those worlds and blurs the other. This is enough to make any man uneasy, who cannot fall back upon a higher, broader positive authority to vindicate his decision.

The politician is the secular man writ bold, and from his example one can learn much. To the contrary of what aristocrats of the spirit allege, the man who is of his times, into whom the passions of the ecumene are poured, is not a mere receptacle or echo box for the despair of the world. He is the field, the chaos out of which the new worlds arise. The aristocrat, on the other hand, who knows with certainty where he has come from, what is valuable, and where he is going, damps out of his soul so much of the saeculum that he cannot be a genuinely ecumenical man but only a representative of a tradition. The aristocrat like the man who sleeps to escape the indifference and self-doubting that seep through all social intercourse is a person whose certainties have transformed him into an object of great interest to others but have also deprived him of sympathy, of the capacities for astonishment, and of the ability to create.

other great fields of human thought and action. He must become the cartographer of the times in his own mind.[18] And if we recognize the propriety of imagining him as a mapmaker whose mission is to survey the religious and other territories of the human spirit in his times, it follows that in projecting the map he will significantly determine the fall of the land in his own being. He has no external guides he can implicitly trust to advise him what is "lower" and profane and what is "higher" and holy. He himself is both the terrain and the scale of projection. This is enough to make any man uneasy.[19]

18. For centuries Christendom pictured the emerging new man as a pilgrim making his way through the world, but the appeal and force of this image resided largely in the tacit understanding that the path of the pilgrim lay through obstacles he had imposed—even if unintentionally—on himself, that pilgrimage was an exercise in self-discovery, self-discipline, self-denial, and self-conquest. The name of mapmaker says more explicitly that the world or worlds through which *homo Christianus* walks belong essentially to his identity. Contemporary philosophical phenomenology explicitly treats the world as an anthropological category. See below, chap. 2.

19. Sartre describes this circumstance as man's "forlornness." See *Existentialism and Human Emotions*, New York (1957), 23 *et passim*. "Man is condemned every moment to invent man." Sartre believes that this state exists because God does not exist. The reality of human freedom and the absence of any divine mandate or decree prescribing just what men ought to do are reverse sides of the same coin. Sartre obviously equates God with a Manipulator or Tyrant and the sense of God with the fearful obedience of the subject living under the authoritarian Being. In this respect, Sartre misunderstands or simply leaves out of account the forlornness of the religious man who knows that his future is not laid out for him simply to actualize but that he must "invent" it, yet in doing so he "invents" not simply mankind in himself but also "invents" the being that God loves. This is what is peculiar about Christian religious forlornness and gives it extra pathetic weight. To know that what one is and what one is becoming are valuable in the eyes of a God who, if he wished, could prefer and create that which is far more perfect, is the essence of Christian forlornness—being resigned on account of freedom to disappoint him (or them) whom one loves and who love(s) oneself. In his autobiography Sartre writes: "God would have managed things for me. I would have been a signed masterpiece. Assured of playing my part in the universal concert, I would have patiently waited for Him to reveal His purposes and my necessity." *The Words*, trans. Bernard Frechtman, New York (1964), 97. But it is the knowing that one has been signed as a masterpiece and left to fill in the canvas oneself that is forlornness for the Christian or any religious man and the thing that gives reality to the presentiment of hell. —Also, Sartre overstates the degree of freedom to invent man. He does not dwell on the fact that the materials of our freedom are part of the given, that we work with what has already been much worked by other men. The problem—and this Sartre understands very well—is that men are endowed with a sense of freedom and of obliga-

The plasticity of our situation demands of the individual that he invent. In fact, the combination of the need with the courage to invent is a chief mark of the man who has assumed responsibility for his secularity. He knows that he has no recourse but to improvise—in at least as radical a way as the great reformers and church statesmen of the fifth, eleventh, and sixteenth centuries.

To invent in the sense required now is, first of all, to come into oneself and to find. What the inventing Christian finds is the fluid relation in which he stands to the institutional matrix of his own religion. The inventor recognizes that he no longer lives "in" the church. He can no longer think of the church as his mother. Analogies drawn from familial life seem hardly adequate in a society whose feature is the great distance that separates the generations. How can the church appear to a man as his mother, when he and his own true parents have become strangers as the times have carried them apart? At best only a few rare persons can sincerely say with Cyprian, Augustine, and Calvin that had they not had the church for their mother, they could not have had God for their father. The very meaning of the preposition for, as a social connective, has altered, because social space and time are no longer fixed.

The same is true of the preposition in. He who wishes to live "in" must now first of all "come in," must imaginatively enter or reenter, even the community that gave him birth. The personal ties that enweb the radial world are not the ties of origin and descent but the ties of adoption. For to the degree that the present age claims us, our like-mindedness with the past, with our own past, attenuates. The result is pain. And when the pain of incomprehension or antipathy abates, too often it gives place to an equally accidental and unreflective nostalgia. Toward the past we live in an oscillation of contempt and homesickness.

---

tion that far overreaches their power. However, religious forlornness is an exacerbation of this sense of responsibility without commensurate power. "Who is my neighbor?" The answer Jesus gives in the parable of the good Samaritan is: Anyone you are indebted to and anyone in need. For the man attuned to telecommunications this means nearly the whole saeculum.

Whoever would live in his own past in a genuine way must imaginatively enter his one-time home ruled neither by nostalgia nor contempt. He must practice this living "in" as an art.[20] The action of revisiting is also an action of self-transformation, an action by the present I of transcending itself. It is an act of autobiography by one who is both the maker and the made. All the while that he is revisiting his birthplace, he is selecting the design in which to place his own past deeds and thoughts and is also choosing those past moments that are recoverable and intelligible, that he feels to be his own in the standpoint of the present. Such living "in" is an act of creating the unity of one's own life—at least for the time being.[21] To be sure, such living

20. Any person who has undertaken the smallest piece of historical investigation knows something about this art. When one lives in another time, by dint of historical effort, he willingly suspends his will, his drive to shape his world, and plunges himself—not uncritically but imaginatively—into that other world already shaped. He disengages his anxiety, as it were, in the face of the moment, to indulge his passions of discovery, astonishment, and understanding. From such acts of time travel, with their temporary respite from the present, he returns enriched. But the same is true of our less artful and considered journeys into the past.

21. Such creating of unity is different from the idea that men must search out their hidden identity or look for the transcendental ego behind the appearances. The task of creating unity in one's life is the task of finding the proper relations among the appearances. No transcendental self or hidden identity comes into question. Comparing Augustine's *Confessions* with a very contemporary diary, Dag Hammarskjöld's, illustrates the difference between these two conceptions of identity. Augustine puzzled over the meaning of his youthful profligacy, but he never imagined that each act was anything less than his own. Even the most reprehensible were still, to his mind, expressions of the reality of his being. See, for example, the chapters of musings on his childish theft of a neighbor's pears (*Confessions*, II, iv-ix). It is only when Augustine perceives that God takes greater delight in the return of a sinner (VIII, iii and iv, for example) that he recognizes also a pattern connecting the moments and appearances of his life as his memory preserves them. Hammarskjöld, on the other hand, writes as follows: "At every moment you choose yourself. But do you choose *your* self? Body and soul contain a thousand possibilities out of which you can build many I's. But in only one of them is there a congruence of the elector and the elected. Only one—which you will never find until you have excluded all those superficial and fleeting possibilities of being and doing with which you toy, out of curiosity or wonder or greed, and which hinder you from casting anchor in the experience of the mystery of life, and the consciousness of the talent entrusted to you which is your *I*." *Markings*, trans. L. Sjöberg and W. H. Auden, New York (1964), 19.

"in" is not an act of absolute creation, ex nihilo. It is an assistance in one's own rebirth. But whoever is not capable or willing to do this much must remain forever outside of every earlier home.

As with our homes, so it is with the other parent communities that survive into the maturity of their offspring and travel parallel courses in time. Individuals cannot both be aware that their life is life in an age rather than a place and live in these societies as their natural dwelling places. They may visit them, come into them, by an act of moral imagination. Obeying the same necessity of inventing, the Christ follower (*homo Christianus*) also does not live in the church as his natural society.

For one thing, the church does not command priority in his consciousness. Unlike his forebears, this man has not received his strongest personality from the great catholic Christian society, and what has come to take its place of primacy in his being is very much his question. He cannot argue with himself, "I join in prayer, therefore I am," because the society of praying men is not antecedently real enough to him. He cannot point to any single birth moment of his self-consciousness. What has come to be first in his mind is the world—not the world of which the Gospel of John speaks as the realm of darkness nor the world as the territory of men and women still unevangelized, but the world as the age of his manhood: the world of beings and actions that pushes against him, invades his thoughts and passions through the great telecommunications system and yet is in no obviously symmetrical relation to his own being and action. The church becomes real to this man as a visible-invisible fellowship only as he becomes a person in his own eyes. But it is difficult for him to collect himself, to pick out the pieces of his own experience that fit each other and add up to a solid sense of being. The autobiographer's work is immense. He has been interwoven into the experiences and passions, the creeds and philosophies of so many other men.[22]

22. He is like the child of which Sartre has recently written: "My truth, my character, and my name were in the hands of others. I had learned to see myself through their eyes . . . . When they were not present, they left their gaze behind, and it mingled with the light. I would run and jump across that gaze . . . . The clear, sunny semblances that constituted my role

How can he then recognize his kindred in the fellowship of the Holy Spirit, when he is so uncertain as to what of himself he ought to re-cognize there?

This is the view that the effort of inventing opens to the radial-age Christian. He is a man belonging to the age as a whole, not only to its light but also to its shadowed scenes, and he is inhabited by its many spirits. He has not necessarily repudiated the church, but it is undeniably difficult for him to feel at home in it. He may listen to the pastoral assurance that man's true nature disposes him toward life in the Body of Christ, but true human nature so often appears much less clearly than do acquired second natures. And the secular man is a being to whom a bewildering variety of second natures is possible. In order therefore to live in the church as a communion building up a new and true humanity, he has to begin by reconstituting himself out of the confused materials his times afford him. He has first to collect himself.

V. Inventing (continued)

The inventing that is a coming in, an act of moral imagination, requires a sister action, that of forming or collecting oneself.

The special romanticism enveloping the notions that Kierkegaard and his followers have dispersed so widely should not distort our perception of this human effort to become one. The man who makes this effort with Jesus of Nazareth upon his mind is not a solitary, heroic artist for whom the church and his own Christianized childhood are merely incumbrances upon his shaping imagination. He is very much a man of the crowd: surrounded by other persons and by mammoth institutions. He is influenced by a history he breathes with every word he speaks. He is also the same man about whom economists, psychologists,

---

were exposed by a lack of being which I could neither quite understand nor cease to feel." *The Words*, 83.

and sociologists write as a consumer, as an id and ego and super-ego, as an other-directed person. Nor is he proudly lonely in his faith or lack of faith, regarding other men's professions of belief or the historical records of the Gospels and the church as un-worthy props arnd supports that threaten to taint the purity of his own existence by faith alone. The warmth of the presence of others is necessary to him. He is already far too isolated and insignificant a creature to repudiate the fellowship available, and he knows that he is a man in whom are reflected and re-fracted the faces and feelings of hundreds of others and untold past generations.

Nevertheless, this individual does share in his own creation—slowly, painfully, and often with only half-formed designs. Such is the free action to which a self-conscious being is constrained, no matter how balked his will may be by habits and laws of his own and of others' making. Such freedom necessitates that he look for a principle of self-government, for a generous pattern to reconcile the various moments of his life.

In this moment of inventing, two vectors rule his mind, the one carrying him away from society and the other toward it. These con-trary motions are familiar in study and research, when men cul-tivate both detachment from, and devotion to, a subject matter. Invention arises in a general sense of intellectual disquiet. It is the focusing of these contrary movements of the mind into a single insight, so that the object of thought appears to the mind's eye through superimposed perspectives and images. As in irony and humor, so here, men raise their discomfort and distractedness to the level of deliberate consciousness to achieve a new way be-tween habitual sympathetic identification with the old order and restlessness, irascibility, and anxiety.[23] Faith too takes new form in a new perception originating in inward distraction and divided-ness.

The inventing of faith is not the fabricating of faith. Religious man can no more fabricate faith than *homo intellectus* can

23. See Arthur Koestler, *The Act of Creation*, New York (1964); also Michael Polanyi, *Personal Knowledge*, 195 ff.

originate reason. Inventing is being witness to the throwing of
a different light upon the familiar. It is realizing that in what
one sees there is opportunity for the witness and his neighbors
to live in a new relationship to their times, to each other, and
to themselves. So the Christian of the radial world invents his
faith. He is compelled to do so, because the Faith of the Church
("what has been believed everywhere, always, and by all") is
an accomplished thing, in which he has no part. Invention is a
necessity to the man whose spiritual equilibrium must—if he
finds it—support an ever-expanding radial world. The cloud
of witnesses to which he looks and is accountable stretches far
beyond the deeds and sensibilities of church-recognized martyrs.
And even the Christian martyrs he remembers epitomize a
human world larger than the church, reflecting the faces of
Jews, Buddhists, Communists, and agnostics. The images and
echoes that seethe in his mind have come into him from the
whole ecumene. A man who shares a common body with his
kind cannot think himself born again, if his rebirth leaves him a
lesser being with lesser loyalties, feebler fellow-feeling, and
immunity to the ills of the saeculum. What he brings to his
meetings and tentative returns into the church fellowship are
not Christian sins but corruptions and weaknesses he shares
with the age. What he requires from this fellowship is not the
diagnosis doctrinal theology provides but a sense of life great
enough to welcome and encompass every spirit that has entered
into the making of his polyglottic soul. To live Christianly is for
him not a matter of adhering to the *corpus Christianum*. To live
Christianly means to him to believe and feel his worlds of motion
pictures and clover-leaf junctions, slaughter in Vietnam, and com-
munions in the Last Supper to be coalescing in his own soul.
If such a man appears to older, settled church Christians as something different from the genus *homo Christianus*, being much too
foreign and light in substance, at least he resembles the nomadic
ancestors of these settled people, who also were once transients,
meandering between captivity and kingdom.

So the man who is representative of his kind invents. As a

pagan he comes upon the church; as Christian or post-Christian he comes into his own pagan heart. Bored with the platitudes of the church, he escapes into the worlds of intellectual, physical, and moral adventure, where the population explosion, the computer revolution, the metamorphosis of education, and the political implosion of the nations upon one another thrust on him endless demands to surpass what men have been and have done before. Disheartened by the weariness and cynicism that grow over him in the thick of these adventures, he rediscovers the simple encouragement that flows through the commonplace confessions of Christian men. He comes upon faith as he lives the meeting of himself with himself. He looks on, as ego and alter-ego spar and probe, admiring the one and defending the other. He experiences the encounter and conflict of his heritages, not as dull pain reminding him of his blindness and profligacy in the "old man" but as the nerve signal of life. This man does not so much care for sanctification as he longs for the justification of all his parts, as vicar and victim of a universe bursting into greater and greater variety. This is our new man. He is molded and informed by many powers, and he is more aware of his own variety than any generation before him. His vocation is to find a definition of his own humanity and so be a shaper of human nature, not disdaining any of the materials given him through and by his generation. Therefore, the whole saeculum, including the post-Christian moods of despair and optimism and indifference toward Christlike virtues, affect him and are part of him, side by side and within his hope, love, and faith. His soul is many, and his faith is not pure. His faith is little, but it would become generous.

chapter 2
Human Faith—Radial World

When Jesus of Nazareth began speaking out for God, he called on his fellows to change their minds in the face of God-Ruling.[1] Since then men have thought and talked much about the new mind that Jesus enjoined, the metanoia excited in the new perception of power that he awakened. For the most part we have come to call this new-mindedness faith—a simple word for a complex reality. But we know that faith is not simple and not something in itself. When faith or faithfulness or new-mindedness appears, it does so in men: men struggling to understand, men wagering on evidence not seen, men fearing, men desiring, and so forth. Therefore, we cannot profitably examine faith as an abstraction from the human mind it qualifies. Our perception never falls upon faith but only upon men in faith attitudes or in faithfulness and states of new-mindedness.

But it is also evident that we cannot find men in the attitudes of faith without also taking notice of the things that prompt and stifle faith. Just as the new mind Jesus portrayed in his parables

1. I use this term to render *basileia tou theou* as the dynamic reality it is represented to be in the Synoptic Gospels.

presupposes the sheaf of wheat, the loaf of bread, the conscription of unwilling guests to a feast, the gesture that stands out like a city on a hill, so the object of our perception is much larger and more complex than merely man in the attitudes of faith. The object is man as a faithful being in his world, standing in an ambience with a visible and determinate character. Of course, these attitudes themselves, particularly as we share them with the beings we observe, are active in our perceiving and defining the character of this enworlding reality; just as this sphere breathes its spirit into our attitudes of faith. Consequently, we cannot tell which of these—faith or world—precedes and sharpens our awareness of the other, nor is it feasible to separate our knowledges of them. But still we must consider briefly each in its turn, our world and our faith.

I. Human World

World may convey a range of meanings in our speech, but whichever of them we are especially intendng for the moment, we are also normally referring to our surroundings, both temporal and spatial, mental and physical; we are referring to the ambience. According to the etymology, the root meaning of world is age of man or man-age,[2] and the ancient prayers that end with the familiar phrase, world without end, illustrate this root meaning. The concept of a world is an "anthropic" concept, one that literally in its origins and tacitly in its usage always includes a reference to the human beings who stand in its midst. The world at hand is *our* world, and any world we speak of is someone's world, never simply a world as such. And what etymology tells us certain recent philosophers have taken up as a motif of their thinking. They speak of the life-world, of the everyday world, of the world that is the opposite pole of self.[3]

2. *Oxford English Dictionary; An Etymological Dictionary of the English Language,* ed. W. W. Skeat, Oxford (rev. ed. 1963); *Origins,* E. Partridge, London (rev. ed. 1963).

3. See Edmund Husserl, *Die Krisis der europäischen Wissenschaften und*

Since each person is a distinctive individual, a peculiar mixture of many elements, so then any world which presents itself to us displays a corresponding idiosyncrasy. Each man, therefore, inevitably lives in a world partly private, but—more importantly—men also share larger worlds, on which their private worlds are dependent. These larger worlds are made out of such elements as common physical endowments, the common earth, a common calendar, a common language, common needs, traditions, aspirations, and moral and political problems. Hence, as each individual moves always in a world, there is, by the same token, always a world that limits him, makes up his horizon of thought and action, that transcends or surmounts him. Perhaps the majority of men and women habitually take their worlds for granted. According to the philosopher Heidegger and the theologian Rudolf Bultmann, such taking of one's world for granted expresses an ignoble and inauthentic style of existence. But this seems to be too sweeping a judgment. For it is clear that all of us do take our shared primary world for granted much of the time and that life together depends on our being able to do so.

The first matter of importance for our thinking then is that whether we have in view mankind or a society or a single person, we perceive such human being existing in a shared world. This world is something much more than the physical earth or solar system which supports life. It is also the historical ambience, the age, of a particular mixture of humanity.

But we want also to know about the kind of world in which faithful man finds himself today. How do we characterize the encompassing age that circulates through his consciousness, modifies the tempo of his body, and shapes the mass of his apperception? Naturally, even the most painstaking descriptions of the present age will falter, since the age is always changing both in its details and principal features. No mortal account could ever exhaust its infinite complexity. There are in reality worlds within

---

die transzendentale Phänomenologie, The Hague (1962); Martin Heidegger, *Sein und Zeit;* and Paul Tillich, *Systematic Theology,* Chicago (1951), vol. 1.

worlds for each man, and he lives usually in more than one of them, sometimes to his relief and sometimes to his acute discomfort. Nevertheless, we are commonly aware of certain elemental traits in the substrate meaning of our shared world for us, which reapper in each of the various individual mixtures of humanity and ambience that make up our generation.

To begin with the most general statement about this world/age, we have to say that what is salient in it is power. It is power in which we live and move and have our physical being. It is power which moves in, with, and under our personalities as we meet and part in this great field of action. It is power from which we flee and to which we run, from which we come and into which we vanish, which we admire and abhor. In our own idiom, we may say that our humanity stands and continually redresses its balance in a radial world. For the individual of this world/age lives in a vortex of rays and waves of light, of sound, of electricity— in short—of particles of energy. To be born is, for this man, to be endowed with power and the conatus for power. To love is to discern and approve the fitting order of powers. To work is to learn a limited management of the power available to one. To die is to succumb to power. In a radial world we have our being as radial men.

Our world, however, is not merely power as such but displays toward, and works on, our humanity in two principal ways: to enlarge us and to make us small. By persuasion and by coercion. Everything which shows itself to us is never only an appearance but is an attracting or repelling appearance, an appearance that enhances and authorizes or diminishes our own being. Our world is therefore never simply with us (too much or too little). It is an intrusive world, an insistent and abrasive world, in every part capable of opposing our intentions, deflecting us from our courses, thwarting our plans, and transforming our purposes. It is also an extraordinary and miraculous world, filling some moments with delight and astonishment. Again, it can be an agreeable world, pliant to our designs and forms. But it is never an indifferent world. It is rather a world that transforms our temporary indifference into hope or despair.

The distinction between coercive and persuasive power is not an ontological distinction. It is rather a phenomenal distinction. We may well suspect or surmise that these qualities originate in an ultimate reality. But so far as our knowledge goes, we can affirm only that it is a distinction men make with a necessity they are helpless to suspend. So coercion and persuasion are qualities of the worldly manifestation of power. Our human world shuts us up (coerces) and opens us toward (persuades) itself. Our lives in turn are a business of reacting—as any being reacts to the power of another being according to the laws of motion—and of responding, that is, animating our reactions with an answering human intention. Jeremiah's angry protest, "thou hast deceived me, O Lord, and I was deceived"; Marcus Aurelius's cultivation of serenity and the death of passion; the existentialist's emancipation declaration that God has given him no script to follow—all of these are expressions of human intentions that have been infused into the perception and awareness that our lives are forever being closed up and set, by laws of motion and change not of our own making, on a course whose end we did not choose before it became our end. Condemnation to prophecy, condemnation to the warfare of reason with the passions, condemnation to freedom are all the work of coercive power. And the greatest human stories are the stories of men who have come to find their condemnation sweet.

Further discussion of coercive and persuasive power belongs to the following chapters. But one point respecting them bears stressing here. It is that persuasion and coercion are not euphemism for good and evil power. For it is not only persuasive power to which men respond because it is good, nor coercion alone to which they unconsentingly react, because it is evil. The values that claim a middle-class American through his birth or education or conversion, such as the ideal of universal education, are attractive, persuasive idea energies, which nevertheless have a coercive effect as they close him up to themselves, determining his life-direction and excluding him from other possible worlds. Similarly to be born is to be subject to a coercion. It is to be thrust into life and implanted involuntarily in a particular society.

But the whole long process of being expelled first from the womb and then from infancy into childhood and finally into maturity and death is a series of coercions to which men may respond.

Our world, then, is an agent-world. Second, this power-world affects us coercively and persuasively. A third trait of the world/age remains now for our attention. This third trait is the social-political aspect of the power that surrounds us. Power ordinarily wears the face of personality—the personality of a charismatic individual or of an institution. The world of power affects men most conspicuously, most dramatically, and most decisively today through the great political, industrial, and military colossae that bestride our earth, imprinting their images on our retinas and sounding their rhetoric in our minds, determining our life-span, modulating our desires, and whetting our appetites for consumption; but also through the great and the demonic personalities of our generations; through the laws, codes, and mores that form our habits; through the universities that exercise our thinking and cultivate our intellectual virtues; and through the motion pictures that stir up and anesthetize our passions. Conversely, the impersonal power we deal with on occasion acts upon us and in us within an arena of encounter that still echoes with the voices and imperatives of these single and corporate personalities.

However, this agent-world is not only social but it is alien. The alien appears and the comparison to the family or the city betrays its inadequacy, when we recognize that any particular world we may have in view is a world of strengths that existed antecedently to the reactions and responses of its inhabitants. Many of the personal forces and moral energies falling on us today were released in another time and have been years or centuries in their traveling through social space and time to reach us, just as the light and sound our telescopic instruments perceive originated when Christopher Columbus set sail or, perhaps, when Israel went into Babylonian exile. The consequence is that any human world is a complex mixture of powers and personal valencies that are not coeval. Some of these elements may be "traditional" yet at the same time too foreign for our sympathetic understanding. Another way of acknowledging the foreignness of the world is to say that for any given generation its world is never entirely a hospitable age of man, for it is always in part an environment of demonic powers secret or known, admirable perhaps but also hostile to human life, impartially confounding our "pretensions to comprehend" and undermining the "moral frame of mind in which one says the real meaning of life is *my* action."[4]

So the world appears to each generation and to each individual as something at least in part defiant of assimilation or even disinterested understanding. In this light it reveals its absurdity. We see that it is absurd in the technical sense of the word, an accidental world containing in itself many reasons that are not reducible to one Reason. And therefore, each agency in the human world manifests, from time to time, a sheer irrationality, which may arouse disgust or admiration, a sense of the incomprehensible givenness or of the free-gift character of things.

The fourth general trait of the world/age—the last we shall mention here—is the intensity of this world of politicized and given strengths as an affecting world, eliciting from its inhabitants generosity and disinterestedness, fear and a chronic sense of tragic conflict at its foundations, an awareness of endlessly intricate proportions and also of humbling contrasts between the familiar and the stupendous.

This radial world is the scene of our moral, physical, and intellectual struggles and triumphs. When men say that a thing is understandable or clear, it is in their world/age or some microcosm of it that its intelligibility and clearness appear. When we affirm that a course of action is right or that a goal is good, both the rightness and the goodness affirmed have their character in this context. When we judge a motion or a line to be graceful, our judgment rests on a history of perceptions of worldly agency. When we move, we engage ourselves with this enveloping field of forces; and whatever things we put together fit one another

4. *The Thought and Character of William James*, 224.

as parts of our world, exhibiting the syntheses and unities it makes possible. But it is also a great dissonant world whose agencies clash and jar one another, making the human consciousness a theater of awarenesses, notions, and intentions that often have no intelligible relation to one another except that they transpire before the same inturned eye and appear to be all happening to the same "me" and "us." As men today reach out through the sciences of nature and through new political instruments such as the United Nations to discover and to shape a cosmos-character in this great world of action, we are increasingly subject to the shock waves of the natural and political environment. Countermotions and energies warp and distend the mind and shatter human projects. Statesmen carefully build alliances to stabilize the age, only to find that hitherto unnoticed fulcrums of power are ready to disturb the background of forces in remoter quarters of the world. New systems of power make for ever new cold wars. The new syntheses of antibiotics, giving a higher pitch of intensity to the biological equilibrium we call human health, create fresh susceptibilities to disease. Men and nations embark on planned courses of action, only to realize that the ground they tread is tilting in quite another direction. Amid such incongruities, to find a balance is no easy business but is won only through the hard practice of generations; and each success inspires a recollection and premonition of other powers always able to upset it. "Upright and firm I stand on a star unstable."[5]

II. Religion

This is the scene, the field, the world of power, in which our human nature appears. It calls for us to recognize ourselves as religious beings and as beings capable of faith.

Although today men are not so easily inclined to regard religion as the seed of divinity in mankind or as the capacity that raises men above the animals, they cannot deny the evidences of reli-

5. Conrad Aiken, *Senlin: A Biography, The Collected Works of Conrad Aiken,* New York (1970), 206.

gion. At least anthropologists, psychologists, sociologists, philosophers, and artists perceive man as a religious being. And so he does in fact appear when we look at human being not as something in itself but as existence and conduct in a world. If we put the matter in its simplest form, man as religious being is man dependent upon and exposed to his total environment and to every element of his world. Religious man is man taking stock of himself, rediscovering that in the survey of self he must contemplate the great world of action in which he lives and moves. Religious man is man recognizing the poverty—indeed the nonsensicalness—of his own being apart from the radial world and concomitantly recognizing the "world of miseries" he carries within himself. Religious man is also man rising from his melancholy sense of exposure to astonishment, to pride, and to humility before the fact of his subsistence in such a world of action in no symmetrical relation to his own actions.

Precisely what religion and man as a religious being are are questions that we today have only begun to answer, and the study of human religion still lies as an immense territory before us. We are now beginning to awaken to scientific self-consciousness about human religiousness as the forerunning generation awoke to the recognition of the universal meanings of human sexuality. But there have already been many pioneers, each of whom has contributed something to our awareness. Religious man is magic-making man (Malinowski), fearing-man (Hume), and man directed toward the Unconditional (Tillich); he is man shuddering before manifestations of the numinous (Otto), devoting himself to and denying himself for the sake of universal ideal-energies (Dewey), like loving and dealing justly and other virtues. Religious man is man feeling his absolute dependence (Schleiermacher), man arrogantly seeking deity and deification (Barth). He is man homesck for a primeval time (Eliade), myth-making man (Cassirer), and man giving himself to transcendent beauty (Jonathan Edwards).[6]

6. Bronislaw Malinowski, *Magic, Science and Religion,* New York (Anchor Books, 1954). The distinction between magic and religion in this discussion

All of these attitudes and kinds of conduct deserve recognition as instances of religion. But we may most simply and succinctly state the link among them all as basic human responsiveness to power. To exist as a religious being is to be awakened from seeing and hearing, from working and thinking, from fearing and desiring to the consciousness that all these actions are affections aroused in us by the presence of power. Human religion is the sense of being aimed at—by strengths coercive and persuasive, which affect men as intellectual beings, as moral beings, as aesthetic bengs, as sentient, and as biological beings.[7] But since all of these qualities of human existence in the world penetrate and modify one another, we cannot identify religion solely with any one of these modes of sensibility. We cannot identify it entirely, for example, with reasoning, be it theoretical or practical reasoning, or with an aesthetic sense, or with the emotions and inclinations of the soul, or with the nisus of biological life toward self-preservation, although man as a religious being includes all these levels of suffering and action. Religion arises as human reaction and answer to the state of being affected totally.

The argument of Friedrich Scheiermacher in his *Speeches on Religion* that religion is neither a special knowledge nor particular morality and yet is inseparably connected with all knowing and moral doing is still a sound statement of human experience. Nevertheless, in order to make religion more understandable to ourselves, we should compare it to some other feature of human

---

collapses. David Hume, *The Natural History of Religion,* ed. H. E. Root, Stanford (1957). Paul Tillich, "The Essence of Religion," *What is Religion?* trans. J. L. Adams, New York (1969). Rudolf Otto, *The Idea of the Holy,* trans. J. W. Harvey, London (1923). John Dewey, *A Common Faith,* New Haven (1934). Friedrich Schleiermacher, *The Christian Faith,* trans. H. R. Mackintosh and J. S. Stewart, New York (Harper Torchbook, 1963). Karl Barth, *Commentary on the Epistle to the Romans,* trans. E. C. Hoskyns, London (1950). Mircea Eliade, *Cosmos and History,* New York (Harper Torchbook, 1959). Ernst Cassirer, *Language and Myth,* trans. S. Langer, New York (1946). Jonathan Edwards, *The Nature of True Virtue,* Ann Arbor (1960).

7. *Afficere, adficere:* to do, to aim at. Hence, to be affected = to be done to, to be aimed at. Skeat, *An Etymological Dictionary of the English Language.*

existence, even though we admit that it is finally sui generis. Schleiermacher tended toward art as his comparative term, choosing such verbs as cultivate and shape to express the active side of religious life. But there is much to be said for Thomas Hobbes, Benedict Spinoza, and the Bible of Jews and Christians, which depict man's religion as something like his politics: as the business of regulating the multiple powers and agencies in the citadel of the self as the self encounters, adapts to, compromises with, and allies its vitalities with the powers and energies that environ it, making up the human world.

What is religion then? It is a quality of man that is unique. But what is it like? It is like politics, for the man who practices the art of politics must know how to balance friend against foe, enforce covenants, exploit the physical situation of his city, promote the health of its citizenry, and plan perspectives leading the eye to the horizon's immensity. He must know how to deal with the entire environing world as a world of power. And as does *homo politicus* so *homo religiosus* shows scientific, moral, aesthetic, and conative moments in his attitudes, because he too exists in a world from which we can isolate and abstract scientific, moral, aesthetic, and psychological elements. But insofar as this human world is none of these things alone but a fusion of all, and insofar as man feels himself to be totally affected, he tries to orient himself within this agent-world as a whole. This perennial striving for orientation in the whole agent-world is human religiousness.

We should add, then, to our description of the world, by observing not only its basic traits of power but also an original effect, which it produces in human beings. It is not only a radial world of coercive and persuasive powers. It is a world in which men seek orientation; and in this need religion forms itself. And where religion appears, the mind is confronted with the genesis of human faith.

But then we ask: What is faith? What kinds of faithfulness does this human world of power and religion breed, tolerate, or encourage? What kinds of faithful or new-minded beings does the

age incorporate? And is this faithful being anything different from
homo religiosus striving but never permanently achieving orientation?

III. *Faithfulness*

Human faith as something effective is not less palpable than the
human environment. It is, in fact, an ascendant energy in the
world. But, sadly for many, the long theological labors of analysis
and dispute have left such a maze of descriptions and definitions
of faith that the quality itself has all but vanished in the labyrinth
of words. Nevertheless, with persistence one can find help in
the history of theological reflection on man as a faithful being.
An acquaintance with Christian theology as a whole indicates that
the majority of close observers have seen faith as something
similar to, though not identical with, a human virtue, a strength
of the mind. Within this general agreement, however, important
differences occur.

Often, for example, men in the tradition of Thomas Aquinas
have likened faith to the inferior form of knowledge Plato called
opinion. They have seen faith as the act of affirming an officially
authorized teaching about God and his creatures.[8] Others have
been more impressed by the parity of faith with intellectual
vision or a direct intuition by reason of the substance or form
founding and shaping the whole world of appearances.[9] A relatively small number of men have associated faith with the mind's
ability to organize sensations and ideas according to some great
image.[10] But all of these parties agree in comparing faith to a
rational virtue.

The action of willing has forcefully suggested itself to others as

8. See *Summa Theologica*, II, II[ae], Q I.
9. See Jakob F. Fries, the neo-Kantian about whom Rudolf Otto wrote,
in *The Philosophy of Religion, based on Kant and Fries,* trans. E. B. Dicker,
London (1931); or Henri Bergson, *The Two Sources of Morality and Religion,* trans. R. A. Audra and C. Brereton, New York (1935).
10. For example, Austin Farrer, *The Glass of Vision,* Westminster (1948).

the best analogy. They have then set faith down as a peculiarly and momentously free assertion, sometimes describing it as the putting of one's trust in the God who is by all the laws of perception and thought beyond nature and the natural; sometimes inflecting this action of trusting so that it appears preeminently as a subordination of self in obedience to a highest will or a universal reason. Modern religious existentialism, deeply impressed by Kant's philosophy of morals and religion, has attributed much weight to these pure moments of decision—willing, choosing, resolving—that reach beyond all sight and judgment.[11] Still other post-Kantian philosophers of religion have stressed in faithfulness the quality of freely given loyalty and fidelity.[12] The late Paul Tillich, in distinction from nearly all of these other modern figures, assimilated faith to a disposition of mind combining the inclination of the practical intellect toward action with the intuitive capacity of contemplative reason in an encompassing state of concern—a notion reminiscent of the biblical perception of man as a caring being.[13]

The first-named group of theologians perceived faith as a virtue of reason; the second as a virtue of willing. Both recognized it as intellectual or mental virtue,[14] and in each of them we still catch sight of something familiar. Yet, neither of these views comprehends man as a faithful being as we know him in our world. We are conscious of an excess in our perceptions of faithfulness that

11. See Søren Kierkegaard, *Philosophical Fragments,* trans. D. F. Swenson, Princeton (1946); *Concluding Unscientific Postscript,* trans. D. F. Swenson and W. Lowrie, Princeton (1944); *Training in Christianity,* trans. W. Lowrie, Princeton (1947); also Rudolff Bultmann, "The Crisis of Faith," for example, in *Essays, Philosophical and Theological,* trans. J. C. G. Greig, London (1955).

12. See "Essay on Faith," *The Collected Works of S. T. Coleridge* ed. Shedd, New York (1854), vol. 5; Gabriel Marcel, "Obedience and Fidelity," *Homo Viator,* trans. E. Craufurd, Chicago (1951); H. R. Niebuhr, *Radical Monotheism and Western Culture,* New York (1960).

13. See Tillich's discussion of ultimate concern in his *Systematic Theology,* vol. 1, 11 ff.

14. Even those who oppose faith to the natural operations of the mind, e.g., to reason, use the intellectual virtue to define what they mean. Often the anti-intellectual becomes the most tightly bound prisoner of his adversaries' formulae. Kierkegaard's imprisonment in Hegel's ideas is an example.

these ideas do not organize and, correspondingly, of a poverty in these ideas.

But, then, we need not think that human faith is changeless. In fact, we know that men suffer changes in their nature, just as our human worlds change; and that there is a time for holiness of life in communion with holy persons and holy things, and there is a time to sin boldly, trusting in predestination and the grace of perseverance. And neither individuals nor generations can choose these times. Their times are visited upon them. We may suppose, then, that faith also is not immutable but changes with us and our worlds. What seems to be true, therefore, is that man as a faithful being is not one thing only but is a being-in-process or a becoming, exhibiting and exercising a many-sided strength that is an elemental force of his nature, enlarging, enlivening, and intensifying his daily world and his own actions within that world.

This evidence suggests that faith, like courage, wisdom, or any other cultivated strength, is not only comparable to the working of distinctly formed capacities of human nature, to the willing of "the will," or the striving of "reason" for knowledge. We also need to compare it to a man's whole way of behaving, of going out of himself and returning. It includes his whole method of taking hold—intellectually, morally, and aesthetically—of the known and "paying deference to the unknown."[15] The language of classical theology offers us a word: a man's faith is his persona, the character, the role, or the discipline to which he submits himself and makes the principle of his self-government. It follows then that what a man is shows in some measure (to those who are watchful) in his faith or faiths. By the same logic, what he may become is foreshadowed in the varieties of personas which are nascent in him and in his times. So that in choosing the mixture of his faiths he is choosing his own destiny. Yet we know that no man may simply choose his faith. He does not have such disposal over his own life-course, for he has his being in a world that resists him while it affects him.

15. From Robert Oppenheimer's paragraph on style in *The Open Mind*, New York (1955), 54.

To say that a man's faith is his persona means nothing shallow or superficial about the being we call faithful being. Men are the ways they act: toward themselves, toward other men, and toward all that is other than themselves. Naturally, the scope of human being does not exhaustively express itself in the visible method of a man's physical, verbal, and emotional conduct. Nevertheless, his method of conduct is part of the man himself and an important part, whether it be a transient or an enduring role. For the function of human being to which the name persona applies is the more or less articulated set of mental and verbal, emotional and bodily manners and habits in and through which a man possesses himself and exercises his share in the total human world.

If religion in experience is the feeling of being totally affected, of being set upon behind and before, within and without, and the striving for orientation in the agent-world as a whole; then human faithfulness presents itself as the great personal act or course of actions in which a man, or some family of men, commits and aligns himself to the one coercive and persuasive power in the world that is the recapitulating expression of the meaning of the whole. So wherever and whenever we see men giving themselves for that which is greater than themselves and greater than all the particular forces impinging on them, there we meet faithful human being.

Something of the difference between religion and faith appears in the contrast between two versions of a certain versicle in The Book of Common Prayer. To the petition, "Give peace in our time, O Lord," the 1550 service of Evening Prayer responds: "Because there is none other that fighteth for us," while the liturgy of the 1928 revision replies: "Because there is none other that ruleth the world." In the first version, apparently, it is the weakness and insecurity of the supplicants in a world of turbulent forces that moves them to address God as a power on their side in the warfare of life. In the second version it is confidence in a single tendency of all energy, in a Governing Power, that prompts the prayer.

The difference between human religion and human faithfulness is one of attitude and scope of reference. Religion intensifies the problem of power in the human world through the peculiar way in which it expresses the feeling of being totally affected. It intensifies the question—or, better, the state of mind from which the question rises—that is asked either directly or indirectly in a hundred forms: Which of these attacking and soliciting energies of the ambience is virtue in itself? Is Logos or Law of Nature the primal strength? Do love and harmony move all things? Is freedom, pure mathematic beauty, or glory the highest good? Which of them is essential power offering liberty from the turbulence and flux of the field of power as a whole? Religion asks: At what in me or in my kind does true power chiefly aim? Myths, cultic practices of sacrifice and prayer, and many other human actions—not least the actions universities cultivate—bespeak these questions. This religiousness is, perhaps, not only the "why" of men seeking death in holy warfare for Allah but also the "reason" that men renounce society for contemplation, choose membership in some elite corps of scientists, or profess willingness to be damned for "my country right or wrong." They have discovered a share in the most persuasive, powerful power of all.

But faithful man has taken another step into his world and himself, asking: How may I play my part in this field of powers? How may I be freed so that I may be aimed in the direction in which all true power and virtue move?

Clearly, religion and faithfulness stand in no absolute antithesis. Both appear within human being in our world of energy and action. And neither one evidences itself without the other as background. We might agree that religion is the naïve form and faith the more self-conscious, self-critical form of man's striving for orientation in the agent-world transcending him.[16] But it is plain that the spirit which breathes in men's minds as it pleases

16. Alfred North Whitehead distinguishes between expressive, emotional religion and universal, reflective religion. His language has the advantage of better preserving the relation between the phenomena here named religion and faith, but it is more convenient to use these two familiar words than Whitehead's circumlocutions. See *Religion in the Making*, New York (1926), chap. 2.

enlivens them in their "naïve" religious moments as well as in moments of faithfulness. And it is plain that the traces of the acts of faith that other men have made before, or we ourselves in times past, give patterns to our religious orientation of the present, either persuasively or coercively. For example, the people who faithfully persevered in years of adversity because of the promise that they should finally posses a land helped to create for their descendants a religion of nationalism, which emerges in times of international struggle. Faithful adherence to a covenant became socially enforced assent to the sentences of the law. Again, the total devotion of Puritan preachers to divine wisdom in Scripture and nature transmuted itself in the passing generations into a religion of reason itself, a religion of intellectual elegance and polite manners among the fellows of the colleges they founded.

Hence, the naïve and sophisticated worlds of religion and of faith are always coalescing and reshaping each other; and there is not—nor has there ever been—a simple world of either religious conduct and language or of faithful knowledge and self-surrender. The consequence is that if the human world is one in which religion is always arising in the perception of power, some element of earlier faithfulness is usually actively present, informing the perception itself. Conversely, if religious sensibility did not sharpen and intensify our perception of the human world as a field of power attacking and persuading us, men would not make the conscious, faithful dedications of themselves to justice or to love or to glory as the power that governs and preserves all lesser energies.

IV. Faith and Affection

These observations of religious and faithful man bring us to a vantage point at which we can better understand our sense of lack in the two descriptions of faith that theologians have customarily offered. Both the concept of faith as a virtue of reasoning and the concept of faith as an exercise of willing are too little appreciative of the nature of our world as a world always inflicting passion. Both of these descriptions slight the fact that faith, however it finally develops, is first of all an awakening of the human mind to the character of power impinging on it. They ignore the nature of faithful man as a suffering being. For if faith issues as an intellectual vision of truth, it begins as an awakening of the mind to its own suffering of the sentiment of reason under the weight of the logical character of the power-world. If faith makes itself public as an act of decision or obedience, it begins as an awakening of the mind to its own suffering of an interest in the highest good under the persuasion of the goodness (the generosity and beauty) of the power-world. The traditional characterizations of human faith do not err in attributing to faithful man a heightened sense of intellectual activity or a keener and more fateful sense of his own decisions; they err rather in omitting the abiding geneses of these actions in the awakening of the mind as such to its own suffering and to the world that makes it suffer.

Therefore, we need a third way of describing faithful man. This third way should not eclipse what the other two make visible but provide depth of view and dimensionality to the figure of faithful man in a radial world. This third way discerns faith as passionate, as a mood, as an affection or attunement of the whole mind and self. The third way apprehends faith in its births and rebirths as a form of suffering in our world of coercive and persuasive power, which suffuses all our individual actions of thinking and willing and endows them with a unifying method and tone.

To help ourselves to understand what appears in this third approach, we need to look more closely at the distinctive features disclosed in this view of faith. The first of these prompts the description of faith as awakening. The New Testament's descriptions of the changed mind and the new birth come to mind here. As new birth of the mind or awakening, faith is a fresh receiving of, and engagement with, the whole human world. In the Gospels of the New Testament faith appears as an experience of (an undergoing) and then as a resultng conviction of the beauty of the enworlding field of powers and strengths and almost simultaneously as a bitter realization of the import of blindness to that beauty. The faithful man the Gospels sketch is the man coming to see and to hear what is there, around him.

The second distinctive feature appearing now is the suffering character of faith. What we view here is much more than pain and sorrow. It is the fact that the awakening, the new mind, overcomes the individual; it befalls him, surprises him. And this surprisingness is not just a passing, superficial moment. Whenever the individual becomes self-conscious in his faithfulness, this characteristic reappears. Faith overcomes him and hence he suffers in it, irrespective of the remorse, gladness, or amazement with which a man greets this accident.

The third feature is the scope of this suffering faith. It is able to endow the individual's thinking and acting with a unifying tone, because it suffuses the entire mind. In the frame of mind that is faith men perceive meaning not merely in patches or in special sacred objects. "In faith," as Dag Hammarskjöld wrote in his journal, ". . . everything . . . has a meaning,"[17] which is to affirm not that all meaning is plain but that there is nothing intrinsically meaningless. No special thoughts and concepts alone carry truth, but every act of consciousness is an act of discovery and every deed an act of creativity.

But we have said enough now to indicate that according to this third way of conceiving and describing faith it is an elemental form of experience. It is an exodus from sleep into the power-world that environs us and shapes us. It is what men once called a religious affection.

The word affection is nearly obsolete now, but its meaning is not. It points to an element of our make-up somewhat similar to that which ancient, medieval, and Renaissance men called the humors of the body: an affection determines a man's disposition or temperament by qualifying all of his perceiving and thinking. The psychology of affections differs from the doctrine of the humors, however, by not positing a purely physiological basis. The

17. *Markings,* 165.

meaning of affection as eighteenth-century philosophers used it and as we are using it here can be more easily identified if we distinguish it from another staple item of philosophical, theological, and literary psychology, the passions.

The term passion as we find it, for example, in Spinoza's philosophical psychology refers specifically to the events in the mind of a man—such as fear or envy—whose causes he does not fully understand. It is fair to say that passion in Spinoza's *Ethics* is usually a "dark passion"; it is a symptom of human disorder and is the equivalent of dumb-suffering,[18] whose only remedy is the opposing enlightened affection, the intellectual love of God. Passion, then, is the name for particular mental attractions or repulsions, especially those that express distance, tension, and turbulence between the self and the environment.[19]

Affection, however, refers to a much more encompassing phenomenon of the life of the mind in the body, a phenomenon that the German language designates by the word *Stimmung*,[20] which the English language can best render as attunement. The attunement of the self is the basic and all-including frame of mind that

18. *The Ethics,* pt. III, prop. I. The word Spinoza used is *affectus,* rendered as emotion in the R. H. M. Elwes translation, New York (Dover Publications, 1955), and as passion or affect in the W. H. White translation, *Spinoza,* ed. J. Wild, New York (The Modern Students Library, 1930).

19. Jonathan Edwards makes such a distinction between passion and affection in his *Treatise Concerning Religious Affections, The Works of Jonathan Edwards,* vol. 2, ed. John Smith, New Haven (1959), 98. See also James Hillman's discussion, *Emotion: A Comprehensive Phenomenology of Theories and Their Meanings for Therapy,* chap. 12. Samuel Taylor Coleridge exemplifies the distinction: "O! if Love . . . sanctioned Desire (or rather, as the rising Sun shoots thro' and saturates with rich light the cloud that veils it, took up and transfigured Desire into its own Being) then, then I should appear as such as I should always be—with the genial warmth of Life, not the Heat of Fever, with the tranquil Vigor of Affection fed by Affection, not the paroxysms of Passion disquieted into Appetite by Fear of Transiency, and the uncertainty as to a correspondent attachment." *Inquiring Spirit, a new presentation of Coleridge from his published and unpublished writings,* ed. Kathleen Coburn, New York (1951), 62.

20. See Otto Bollnow, *Das Wesen der Stimmungen,* Franfurt am Main (3rd ed., 1956); Martin Heidegger, *Sein und Zeit,* chap. 5; Leo Spitzer, *Classical and Christian Ideas of World Harmony: Prolegomena to an Interpretation of the Word "Stimmung,"* Baltimore (1963); and *Friedrich Schleiermachers Aesthetik,* ed. R. Odebrecht, Berlin (1931), 48 ff.

gives to the whole of personal existence its determinate quality, color, and tone. An affection, so conceived, is not a specific response to a stimulus or object, although a particular object may elicit in us a consciousness of the pervasive tone of our existence. Rather, it tempers the rapid succession of stimulae and responses in personal existence and superimposes on them a degree and quality of order. According to this way of viewing man, both the transmitting and transmuting of incentive from the world to the kinesis of individual life are functions of the tonality and intensity of our affections.[21]

Another term that has been often employed for the same phenomenon is resonance, a word that also conjures up musical and mathematical associations.[22] But whatever the name be that we give to this phenomenon of personal existence, whether tonality, resonance, attunement, or affection, the corrective implied by all this nomenclature remains clear: it is not sufficient to conceive of faithful man in the world as a rational soul, nor even as rational being whose dignity lies in choosing or willing. He is also an affectional being whose thinking and willing are themselves always qualified by the specific affection or resonance that pervades the whole person-world polarity. To ignore this affectional dimension of personal existence is to commit a psychological reduction that

21. See, for example, The Earl of Shaftesbury, *An Inquiry concerning Virtue or Merit, Characteristicks of Men, Manners, Opinions and Times*, London (4th ed., 1707), vol.2. "It might be agreeable," Shaftesbury writes "one would think to inquire thus into the different Tunnings of the Passions, the various Mixtures and Allays by which Men become so different from one another." (95 f.) Edwards reflects a similar view of the mind, emphasizing the passions and affections as the motion-supplying connection between man and his world; see *Treatise Concerning Religious Affections*, pt. I. Raymond Klibansky, Erwin Panofsky, and Fritz Saxl provide a fascinating history of the psychological concepts involved here, in *Saturn and Melancholy: Studies in the History of Natural Philosophy, Religion and Art*, London (1964).

22. By its particular state of attunement, the soul is so constituted as to dampen or amplify the signals that vibrate in its environment, and so, in effect, a man's inner affectional condition or resonance qualifies the character of the world in which he moves. See Richard Woltereck, *Ontologie des Lebendigen*, Stuttgart (1940), 15 *et passim*; also Herbert Read, *The True Voice of Feeling, Studies in English Romantic Poetry*, New York (1953), 184 ff.

in turn leads to a misinterpretation of human faith in its radial world.

The possible extent of such misinterpretation becomes more evident, if we make explicit still another feature of affection, which we have not yet developed in our interpretation of this element of man's faithfulness. A true affection lies at such a depth in personal existence that it is inaccessible to volition. So much is clear from the fact that it is affection that endows the will with its specific tone and energy. This givenness or fatality of affection, which is consonant with the experience of faith as a frame of mind thrust on oneself, shows strikingly in the journals of David Brainerd, an early eighteenth-century missionary to the Indians in the American wilderness.

Lord's Day, Dec. 9 [1744]. Preached, both parts of the day, at a place called Greenwich, in New Jersey, about ten miles from my own house. In the first discourse I had scarce any warmth or affectionate longing for souls. In the intermediate season I got alone among the bushes, and cried to God for pardon for my deadness; and was in anguish and bitterness, that I could not address souls with more compassion and tender affection. I judged and condemned myself for want of this divine temper; *though I saw I could not get it as of myself, any more than I could make a world.*[23]

Brainerd states that he could no more obtain the "temper" he longed for by his own efforts than he could create a world.

We are now able to gather together the main points in this third way of describing faith in the context of the general understanding of man in his world in the following theses: Self and world form a polarity or binary. In order to render concrete personal experience we must not only take account of the fact that men have their being in a radial world but also recognize that they continually seek orientation in the field of their existence and fall into ways of seeing and of conducting themselves that amount to faith. However else we interpret faith, we must make room in

---

23. *Memoirs of the Rev. David Brainerd; Missionary to the Indians: Chiefly Taken from his own Diary;* ed. Jonathan Edwards and Sereno Dwight, New Haven (1822), 182. Emphasis added.

our minds for its affectional character. Affective faith is an awakening, a suffering of a whole frame of mind that endows the individual with a resonance lying at the foundations of his existence. It qualifies all of his interaction with other men, with himself, and with his near and ultimate environment.

Different observers have put the intimate relation between affection and faith or religiousness in varying ways. One contemporary phenomenologist writes:

What moves [man] most deeply is personal existence; his relation to other persons, to the world as the "place" of every real and possible personal existence, and to transcendence as the reality that makes the understanding of personal existence possible . . . no convincing interpretation of [the "heart" (*Gemüth*)] can be expected from a purely humanistic philosophising . . . . To speak of feeling, heart (*Gemüth*), emotionality, passionateness and not intend thereby to take seriously the essential religiousness of man would be a self-contradicting enterprise.[24]

To the sixteenth-century pastor and theologian, the affectional dimension of human nature appears as an indispensable element in the definition of Christian faith as being not only a knowledge of God's goodness but a knowledge "*revealed* to our *minds* and *confirmed to our hearts* by the Holy Spirit." For as John Calvin put it:

Faith consists in knowledge of Christ [as the visible promise of God]. Christ cannot be known without the sanctification of his Spirit. Consequently, faith is absolutely inseparable from a pious affection.[25]

The most concrete and acute understanding of faith as affection, however, comes to us from a man who stands historically midway between Calvin and the contemporary phenomenologist of the soul, namely, Jonathan Edwards.

Such is man's nature that he is very inactive, any otherwise than he is influenced by some affection, either love or hatred, desire, hope, fear or some other. These affections we see to be the springs that set men

24. Stephen Strasser, *Das Gemüth*, Utrecht (1956), xiv.
25. *Institutes of the Christian Religion*, trans. John Allen, Philadelphia (no date), III, II, viii.

agoing, in all the affairs of life, and engage them in all their pursuits . . . . We see the world to be exceedingly busy and active . . . take away all love and hatred, . . . affectionate desire, and the world would be, in a great measure, motionless and dead . . . .

And just as the affections define the character and the direction of a man's life—for which phenomenon Edwards uses the term heart—so they also, Edwards goes on to say, animate the heart with a "lively and powerful" religion. Edwards does not argue that the word affection is interchangeable with religion or faith. The point is, rather, that without affections there can be no "true religion." There may be an idea of God but not a relish or fear of his presence, his majesty, and beauty. Edwards puts it:

There are multitudes that often hear the Word of God, and therein hear of those things that are infinitely great and important, and that most nearly concern them, and all that is heard seems to be wholly ineffectual upon them, and to make no alteration in their disposition or behavior; and the reason is, they are not affected with what they hear.[26]

V. Distraction and Simplicity

The benefit of attending to Edwards, to Calvin, and to other careful interpreters of our nature, like Spinoza, is the sharpening of our perception and the widening of our understanding of human faith. But their observations give us no authority to conclude that all men must finally be recognizable as beings of this or that kind of religious orientation, let alone faithfulness. The complexity of our age and the scale of the changes that have intervened between the Reformation and the present deny that recourse to us, in any case. The authority we may reasonably look for, rather, is that of present experience laid open and made readable by a more empirical and less dogmatic view of religion and faith. We look for the authority to acknowledge the significance of what is presented to us: the experience of faithfulness

26 *Treatise Concerning Religious Affections,* 101 f.

as a way of behaving and holding oneself in our world not only as thinking, assenting being or as willing, choosing, desiring being, but also as affective, suffering being. And, we believe, experience does confirm that our humanity is affective being, even in its fleeting existence as *homo Christianus*.

The recognition of this actuality does not, of course, strip faithfulness of its difficulties: either the difficulties of living in it or the difficulties of understanding it. What it does accomplish is to transpose the key in which we carry out our interpretation of human faithful existence. It transposes the key in which we understand how men awaken in their world (if they do awaken), how they become new-minded (if a new mind is thrust upon them). We have still to inquire, however, what such awakening today involves, what it includes of the content of past faithfulness, particularly of the faithfulness of earlier Christian generations.

In what seems now a time long ago (but reckoned linearly is only yesterday), poets and philosophers of Europe, England, and America liked to say that every man is a compendium of the human race, an epitome of history. To the Romantics this insight offered promise and inspiration in an era when men were only beginning to suspect the actual variety of human nature. But what to these poets and philosophers was a source of wonder and excitement has become nowadays a cause of distraction. For richness is also confusion. Universality is also manyness. The knowledge that each man is many is a burden.[27] If we feel ourselves to be close in spirit to any of our forerunners who similarly knew the multiplexity of man, it is closeness not to Schlegel, Schelling, or Coleridge and their Shakespeare but to that man in the cemetery of the Gerasenes who said, "My name is Legion." The experience and endurance of this inner manyness has stirred in our generations a pathos for simplicity. Plainness of language is what our philosophers pursue; simplicity of statement arouses in the scientist his noblest emotions; angular lines mark our architecture. Among men of religious sensibility there is a growing deep admiration of economy. To be sure, we live in the midst

27. Chap. 1, sec. II-V offer a description of this manyness.

of great plenty. But the desire to be one and nothing more prompts some to put away goods and others to distrust attachment to the spiritual possessions of the past as unbecoming and destructive. The preference is to "travel light" and to discard whatever possible, certainly all that seems inane. For some men the idea of God is among these inanities.

The situation of the man still exercising or seeking a Christian method is not significantly different. He too is attracted by simplicity, yet knows that he is compounded of innumerable elements. If anything, perhaps, he is even more self-consciously aware that he lives among ruins of the past, which tower around him and thrust up through his mind. Indeed, psychiatrists, sociologists, intellectual historians, and our other archaeologists of the soul have made him incurably aware that his own thoughts and emotions rest on the religious debris of other men's histories. They have also shown him how from time to time—through some erosive action—the buried past reappears and becomes an accidental part of the present. Then this Christian asks himself, as he gazes on these monuments without and within: Am I responsible to these ruins of past belief? Are they a part of myself? Or are they rather relics?—to be preserved, perhaps, though they are incapable of reanimation.

chapter 3
Believing

I. The Burden of the Past

Remembering makes a dilemma for us. If we allow the past to obsess us, we forsake our freedom and obligation to the present and the future. If we carelessly forget it, we bring calamity on ourselves.[1] The children of a Freudian culture live in fear of forgetting—and of knowing too much.

1. So widely do men believe this, that the premise of one recent apology for Christianity, John Baillie's *Our Knowledge of God*, New York (no date), is that no modern man can willingly divest himself of Europe's and America's Christian past and so invite spiritual sickness. Therefore, the argument runs, this individual needs to appropriate self-consciously the faithful ways in which his fathers conducted themselves. He needs to do this for his health's sake; otherwise the vestiges of their spiritual habits of faith will lie decaying in his soul and poisoning his whole being. Baillie follows in this book a very general Augustinian pattern of thinking. But whereas Augustine dwelt upon the mind's recollection of eternity, Baillie has transferred the recollection to the temporal plane. While much in this book is most attractive, the argument does not entirely succeed. For many a contemporary is free and ready to say that, whatever inner discomfort he may experience, he feels no sting of conscience to make himself in the image of his forebears or of his forebears' faith. The Christianity of the

An impartial observer of the times would surely notice many inconsistencies in the attitudes and interests of present generations toward their own moral, social, and historical origins. Some moments in the long, long times of our making fascinate men today with an almost inexplicable appeal, so that no amount of time, labor, or care is too great to penetrate their mystery. "This is the point," they say while referring to the era of the 1920's or to World War II, "at which we were shaped. Here we can see what we are in essence, newborn and unencumbered by perverse, unnatural, or hypocritical mores." Other moments we reject as accidental to the process of our becoming, cautioning ourselves against the fallacy of reasoning genetically.

Such inconsistency is only to be expected, however. It is the outcome of the selectivity of our interests. Nevertheless, a serious dilemma reveals itself here. As our human productivity increases, particularly our productivity of information about our race's history and our own cultural and personal origins, there grows in the individual an ever more apparent restiveness before the goods of self-knowledge. The mass of our culture closes the human spirit in a tomb of information and theory as well as of material goods.[2] And men are forced to ask how they may liberate themselves.

One age-old way of freeing oneself from unwanted self-knowledge is forgetting or suppressing what one does not wish to remember. Today this way is not open to us who have been prevented by the warnings of psychiatric medicine. Nevertheless, among the hardest problems is that of choosing what not to regard as essential or appropriate, choosing what to forget in the sense of relegating it to the archives of microfilms and electronic

---

past did no doubt shape the lives and conduct of our predecessors and so has left its mark on their legatees through the indirect influence of their cultural legacy. But men who accept the present as their own responsibility cannot honorably surrender their obligation to direct themselves and their own generation in new ways, merely to avoid increased personal tension and strain.

2. See Ernst Cassirer's essay, "The Tragedy of Culture," *The Logic of the Humanities,* trans. C. S. Howe, New Haven (1961), 182 ff.

memory banks, in order that men may be free to comprehend whatever in their past and present is urgent to their immediate future.

It does little good, therefore, to admonish a generation and its members about their Christian tradition. Tradition as such is of small importance to men struggling to re-create, preserve, and direct their humanity. For the things that arrest our attention are not so much what our progenitors have tried deliberately to hand on to us as that which circumstances compelled them to make of themselves and so to reveal of human nature. In turn, what most forcefully impresses itself on us, as we observe ourselves in this time, is not that we do the things our fathers learned to do, but that we must learn again—and often for quite different reasons—to do the things they did.

What then do we see in radial man? How shall we understand his method of sharing in the economy of power, as he examines himself in this man-age and considers the age as it flows through his life? What is his relation to the faith that is still symbolized and embodied in the surrounding monuments of earlier Christian life? Does he make these monuments his home? All that we have observed declares that he does not and cannot. Here too he does not live "in" but lives toward and away from these past patterns of faithfulness, like a planet standing now in perigee and now in apogee in its revolutions about the sun. Clearly, radial man is not a citizen of a Christian "cosmos." But we want to know what sort of wanderer he is in his time-space. What are the special ways in which he feels himself to be aimed? And how does he conduct himself in his radial world?

As we have seen, the ways of faith for which men have borrowed the name of Jesus have carried different though not unrelated meanings. And we have noticed how faith often appeared to pastors and teachers of the Christian life as a special operation of intellect or of willing.[3] But since all readings and analyses of faith depend for their validity on the actual features which faithful conduct presents, we are always obliged to look again at what

3. See above(chap. 2, sec. I.

we wish to describe. In doing so, we have seen one other configuration of faithfulness, which is especially significant—a configuration not utterly new either as a whole or in any of its elements but new to our understanding of what is involved in faithful living and sharing in our age. This third way of seeing faith employs a perception less defined by theological tradition and more attuned to our own context: the agent-world of coercive and persuasive powers. The third perception is of human faith in the fundamental polarity of pathos and power. Faith, then, is like a passion or a mood or affection.

Faith of this sort appears chiefly in three forms: first, in the mind as it inquires, reflects, and judges in company with other persons; second, in the mind as it perceives and attends to the powerlessness of human being; and, third, in the mind as it meets and newly discovers its own being with the being of others in this great field of action. In all of these appearances faith displays an affectional character, which theologians as a class have little noticed since the eighteenth century. But we in our radial world, where powers persuade and coerce us, are well qualified to recognize this character of faith. For it is in faithfulness that men bear power, seek a share in power, and themselves become directed and powerful. In this chapter we shall look at the first of these forms, believing, and in chapters 4 and 5 at the second and third forms respectively, namely, fear and joy, and conversion or awakening.

II. Believing

A species of human faithfulness appears within the large and complex activity of our making intellectual judgments. Augustine long ago noticed and examined the believing and trusting which profit—indeed, are indispensible to—human inquiry and understanding.[4]

All of our thinking that involves a combining of perceptions and

4. See *On the Profit of Believing, Basic Writings of St. Augustine*, ed. W. J. Oates, New York (1948), vol. 1, 414 ff.

statements exhibits a motive power, which is itself distinguishable from the perceptual and logical elements being combined. Part of this motivation is, no doubt, the universal human hunger to "know" the real by achieving the closest possible identification with it. An eros drives our reasoning. Another part is the desire to find efficient means to accomplish the ends men have in view. Practical wisdom or expediency as well as love of being moves us onward and together as intellectual beings. But a significant contribution to this motivation arises specifically from the *relying* of men on the testimony of other men and on their own powers of observations and synthesis. Other men's perceptions, their combinings of their perceptions, and their acts of knowing in general exercise an attractive power on us. The attraction may show itself to us and work on us through the austere self-control a scientific method imposes on its practicer, or through the "elegance" of the conceptual models the scientist creates.[5] It may operate more spontaneously through the character of the other perceiving, knowing agent. In any case the mental actions of others elicit from us a desire to share *their* judgments and bind them to our own, to enrich ourselves with *their* experience as fitting to our own, to enlarge our world with *their* perspectives and horizons. This being attracted is a passion of the mind, and this passion is the passion of believing.

To say that believing is passionlike in character is not to affirm that it is irrational or that ideally it has nothing to do with our acts of choosing and deciding. Rather, what is at stake here is simply the recognition that believing, even though it accompanies thinking and choosing, is not entirely the product of an act of judgment or an act of choice. To be sure, in retrospect any given instance of human believing may appear to be the product of logic alone. But that is due to the fact that a similar kind of believing accompanies our reasoning today. Again, certain instances of human believing may appear arbitrary, but that is due to the fact that today our believing accompanies and reinforces different sorts of choices.

5. See Michael Polanyi's description of believing in the sciences: *Personal Knowledge,* chaps. 6 and 7.

Believing does not figure obviously in all our thinking. There are apparently some acts of knowing which rest on no other grounds of certainty and valuation than the immediate impersonal and even apersonal clarity of what is apprehended and thought. Philosophers have frequently cited mathematics as the conspicuous example of such knowledge, though some mathematicians disagree with them. But such apersonal clarity and enjoyment does not accompany the greater part of our thinking and inquiring. Here, rather, there runs a sustaining and energizing current of beliefulness, which is not the energy of eros in reasoning or the energy of interest and desire in practical thinking. The curious mind, the lover of books for example, exemplifies human nature charged with this eneregy of believing; and it is such moral energy that is the source of the more common and complex or mysterious certainty and enjoyment attending the greater part of our thinking and knowing.

Believing is a distinct activity. It is a response. It is a specific human way of taking hold of the agent-world in which men have their being. In order to discern it, however, we need to distinguish believing from the meaning we usually attach to the word belief. We speak, to be sure, of our deep convictions as our beliefs, but we also often give the name of belief to forms of knowledge such as opinions, surmises, and suppositions, which a strict Platonism or positivism would call weak. Belief covers, in fact, a wide range of degrees of certitude. And many a belief we find in ourselves has long since drifted from the mental energy and larger pattern of activity that produced it. Indeed, we often entertain beliefs while scarcely being aware that our minds are actively engaged at all. So that there is a relatively unconscious or passive holding of beliefs, which is not the same as believing.

The activity of believing as something distinguishable in itself becomes clearer and emerges in its own right, when we recognize that believing is "holding dear" or valuing[6]—but without having

6. The etymology of the word supports this connotation. Its stem is related to the German *lieben* and *glauben*. See Skeat, *An Etymological Dictionary of the English Language*.

or possessing that toward which it is directed. In the attitude of believing, the believer acknowledges that there is distance and separation between himself and the object of his attention. He acknowledges, moreover, that this is a distance which cannot be annulled, so long as the believing continues, for it is the believing itself that preserves the sense of distance. This distancing shows itself most clearly in the activity of holding dear another human being. Even full knowledge of another man, such as that which is in theory at the disposal of the ideal biographer, does not supplant the attitude of believing. On the contrary, believing (or its opposite) checks, governs, and regulates the tact with which the biographer fits together what he knows of the other.

The intimacy of one human being with another is usually in part an intimacy of believing: an intimacy involving a respect for the exteriority and separateness of believer and believed. To believe in a self-conscious fashion is to be aware that believing is the opposite of the desire to own, to infringe, or to restrict the freedom and sublimity of that which is believed.

Believing is thus an original and underived form of valuing with self-restraint on the part of the believer, of admiring with humility. While it appears preeminently in our explicit and tacit judgments of other men, it is also present in the way we manage our minds under the great ideas that govern our thinking, such as the idea of the equality of all men or the idea of the imperishable value of facts. We cannot say that we *have* these regulating ideas, for we subject ourselves to them; we cannot entirely elucidate them from still other elements of our mental world, yet the coherence of that world depends on our relying on them. We hold them dear and bind ourselves to them in the peculiar manner of believing them.

We can therefore only think that holding dear in this way is something natural and indigenous to human nature. Its naturalness, to be sure, does not mean that believing has an organ of its own or appears independently and unaccompanied by other activities. It is natural in the way that the "moral sense" philosophers meant when they spoke of the regard for virtue as a "natural affection" in men. Its absence or weakness leaves the mind dull.[7] It is a specific way in which the mind is affected by persons and ideas and a specific way in which it responds to them without possessing them. Believing is a form of taking hold of the agent-world, of suffering and enduring persuasive power and of governing oneself within it. And if men lack it or are deficient in it, they are miserable in themselves and crippled in their ability to share in any kind of society and its undertakings.

III. Believing and Enlargement

To acknowledge that believing is natural is not, however, to suppose that any given form or style of believing is ineluctable. There is in believing always a conventional character, something acquired and artificial. We can see this in the way that the particular expressions and symbols of believing vary with the times; for example, in one age believing takes recourse to ancient authors, in another it cites living authorities; in one age the symmetry of evidence while in another the properties of simplicity or sensory vividness elicit and direct the energy of believing. Acts of believing and attitudes of beliefulness show the marks of human nurture and culture, so that one might argue with a certain plausibility that human beliefulness has no more than a merely putative moral quality, to which only religious philosophers and theologians find it necessary to appeal. One could, indeed, take even a view modeled on Hobbes's philosophy of con-

7. Hobbes's remark concerning the role in the mind of the passions in general may be applied verbatim to the particular passion of beliefulness. "And therefore, a man who has no great passion for any of these things; but is, as men term it, indifferent; though he may be so far a good man, as to be free from giving offence; yet he cannot possibly have either great fancy, or much judgment. For the thoughts are to the desires, as scouts, and spies, to range abroad, and find the way to the things desired: all steadiness of the mind's motion, and all quickness of the same, proceeding from thence: for as to have no desire, is to be dead: so to have weak passions, is dullness; and to have passions indifferently for every thing, GIDDINESS, and *distraction." Leviathan,* ed. M. Oakeshott, Oxford (1960), 46.

tract and say that believing is only the means by which men establish conventions. Men believe one another, to a point, for believing is the means of making and of employing the tacit compact to be truthful or constant in the use of words and symbols and property in return for the constancy of others. But it is difficult to conceive of any attitude or ability in human nature as being merely artificial and no more. So far as experience has shown us, what men make of themselves they make out of the human nature at hand with its predispositions and limits. In any case, even if human believing—and hence all human society—is artificial is some measure, it is the product of an art that forms the artist, an art in which man becomes Godlike and enacts, as Hobbes has said, "that *fiat* or the *let us make man*, pronounced by God in the creation."[8]

No matter then how small a thing it seems, when we consider it apart from its general context, or how conventional it appears in a certain kind of purely historical view, believing is still the quantum that gives momentum to corporate undertakings and to those labors in which the individual converts his innate need of his fellows into active partnership with them.

And since no simple, fixed boundary divides the conduct of a man toward his fellows and toward himself, we find men directing this energy of believing not only outward but also reflexively. If we rely on the perceptions of other individuals, we rely also on our own and on our memory of them. If we believingly adopt the testimony of others, we similarly affirm, by an act of believing, the reasonableness of our own synthesizing and reasoning.[9] In fact, these two "vectors" of believing, toward other and toward self, energize each other. Each individual is

8. *Ibid.*, 5.
9. William James writing on "The Sentiment of Rationality" is as instructive as he nearly always is. But I think that he has omitted the moral element, the element of valuation in which moral responsibility is involved, when he attibutes the adoption of canons and styles of rationality to "sentiment." James does see the intimate relation between "philosophical interest" and "imaginative Faith." Yet, again, he attributes their differences to "sentimental temper." See *Collected Essays and Reviews,* New York (1920).

forever borrowing the believing of his fellows—in its many-vectored movement toward some object, toward self, and toward colleagues—and then extending his renewed and enlarged (or diminished) confidence toward them again, thereby spinning the skein of human trusting.

Apart from such active believing as this we know that both society—be it the family or the nation—and the individual would be lacking in the most striking, vigorous, and kinetic unity proper to man: the unity we call personal and moral. Where mutual confidence and sense of common allegiance does not prevail among men, there is the distractedness that in nations is anarchy, that in smaller societies such as universities is the sullenness of its students, departments, and administration, and that in individuals is despair and impotence. It is no wonder, therefore, that men need to be always arriving at fresh recognitions of the fact that the human disposition toward beliefulness is an original moral energy infusing our life with much of its élan: an energy that thinking itself cannot produce but only employ and that reflection can admire but not of itself preserve. Such fresh recognitions bring with themselves a sense of the intrinsic value of this energy, its goodness and substantiveness in itself as well as its utility.

Examples of such believing are everywhere within everyday life. Such examples reveal the actual complexity of this normal moral activity. The member of a college, for example (or of any purposive association), meets the biplicity of believing—its utility and its goodness in itself—in his collegial experience. For he finds his place as agent and citizen in a society of co-workers whose labors are founded on the tacit compact to believe and to be beliefworthy. Here the energy of believing is indispensable to effectiveness. All social education and inquiry depend on it. In effect, each man in a society of inquirers covenants to use the language and symbols of the society in a straightforward way. He pledges to restrain his merely private interests for the sake of his contribution to the public work. He swears not to deceive intentionally. Yet he does not in fact pledge, covenant, and swear.

Only a few professions employ public oath. He commits himself silently, perhaps even not in full awareness of the import of his commitment. Yet a profound morality informs and sustains such shared inquiry, a morality that symbolizes itself in the almost spontaneous action of believing. Inquiry could not proceed without it. Here, then, is the social utility of believing, although utility by no means exhausts the value of such disciplined believing. It shines with a kind of splendor that nearly all men admire as something glorious in itself.

But the individual member of such a collegial society of inquirers discovers something else in his participation. He discovers an important element of human dignity, in the following way. He finds that just as he cannot know (in the sense of being able conclusively to demonstrate) that each of his colleagues is restraining his private interests for the sake of the common work, so none of them can know that he too keeps covenant. Each party can only believe—that is, trust and value—the other as one who is keeping covenant. He finds that each member of the undertaking is an original source of believing. Each member is not only what Immanuel Kant called an end in himself but also an originator in himself, a first cause. The individual "has" dignity, because he gives what no other can give on his behalf: respect for such great regulative ideas as the imperishable value of facts and regard for his fellow vessels of such respect. Here believing is no longer simply socially useful. The capacity for believing signifies the capacity of the individual to be a creator and conserver of value, worth, and intellectual and moral energy that will in turn enliven others.

Therefore, taking part in a society in which this energy of believing appears expands, sustains, and dignifies men, enlarges the individual. In the moral kinesis of a fraternity of inquiry and reflection, the individual acquires a larger identity. He is informed not only by a common labor but by a corporate regard for each member as an original source and author of the moral energy of believing, of self-restraint, respect, and reciprocating regard. He acquires the identity and the personality of that society. This larger personality does not displace his persona as an individual. Rather it symbolizes his greater share in human being. The collegial undertakings that display this expansive moral energy extend throughout our society and support its culture. The chemist, as he records his experiment, acts out his presumption of the trustworthiness of his fellows and also an enjoyment of their confidence in him. He is a member of a community of "all sorts and conditions of men" whose common allegiance to the virtues of the scientific mind has made them a brotherhood, each of equal and immeasurable worth. The admiration the great scientific brotherhoods command is well known. These many-colored, international, multireligious fraternities irresistibly attract the man of our radial world, not solely because their systems of law, hypotheses, and procedures impress him as grand or mysterious, nor solely because they are productive organizations, but also because they burn so visibly with the energy of believing. Such societies give a new resonance to the medieval Christian aspiration that all men in all times and places should believe together. They show the passion of believing being trained into a disciplined excellence, a social virtue. This virtue is not only the origin of much of their attractive power but also the bond that makes of their many members one social body and personality.

Beyond the natural sciences there lie less dramatic but more universal instances of the enjoyment and appreciation of believing as something that constitutes and enlarges life. The student of any art or science finds himself enlarged and vivified in his studies by this energy of believing. Something more than a common subject matter draws him into the action of teaching and learning; the affection that the eighteenth-century philosophers called the "love of virtue" comes to rule him.[10] Directed by

10. For an analytical discussion of the fellowship founded on reciprocal love of intellectual virtue, see the Earl of Shaftesbury's *An Inquiry concerning Virtue or Merit,* especially Bk. III, pt. II, sec. I. Jonathan Edwards' *Nature of True Virtue* is the clearest and most precise exposition of the way in which such virtue acts as the principle of unity and motion on both the personal and metaphysical levels.

such a love, men come to prize something that is neither personality alone nor an abstract idea, such as literary beauty or historical truth; they value rather a beauty or a truth appearing in and through the intellectual disposition and moral personalities of their fellows. (Doubt, as an intellectual tool, is an instrument of such believing, as we shall have further occasion to see.)

Finally, these same features of believing appear, even less conspicuously but more importantly, in the most common of all intellectual activities, the reading of books. For reading is not only the attempt to satisfy interest in the information content promised; it is the act of a man who so long as he reads wants to believe in the author's steadfast regard for the intellectual strength and discipline of his reader. The reader wants to value not only the author's expertise (i.e., experience) but also the author's respect for him as a man capable in his turn of authorship. Hence, if there is intellectual pleasure in reading, it arises from the assurance that here there is generosity at work and not deceit: artfulness, perhaps, and wit, satire and cynicism, but not duplicity. The generations who have made the reading of the Bible their lifelong practice have drawn consolation and strength from their reading of it, because of their assurance that the Bible is throughout an expression of constant purpose to be constant toward the reader. To these men and women, the Bible is the book that makes explicit this promiselike character of the complex believing or holding dear that is latent in the use of all words. It is an archetypal word and promise, therefore.[11] It focuses in the devout reader his understanding of the moral unity and substantiveness of his own life and that of his world. And the nowadays seemingly awkward and excessive veneration which some Christians still show toward the literal text of the Bible is, to a degree, the demonstration of their conviction that God

11. Calvin—more than any other theologian of the Bible—defines faith in accordance with this view of word as steadfast promise: "Now [faith] . . . is a steady and certain knowledge of the divine benevolence towards us, which being founded on the truth of the gratuitous promise in Christ, is both revealed to our minds, and confirmed to our hearts, by the Holy Spirit." *Institutes of the Christian Religion,* III, II, viii.

is not a God of deception.[12] These Scriptures have been to these men and women their certificate of franchise in a cosmic society unified not merely by beliefs but by beliefulness or—to borrow Coleridge's phrase—by "fidelity to being."[13]

These examples of believing, in the sciences and in reading, confirm our interpretation of believing as a moral passion. Believing generates in the intensification of mental activity and augments the range and power of our minds and our personas. (Credulity differs from believing as the uncritical or passive acceptance of others' goods differs from active valuing.) When men believe together, they collect themselves around "the believed" and around their common believing, regulating in each his own current of beliefulness and self-restraining admiration. In such believing we have perceived (1) the nature of the believing agent: he is one who prizes and restrains himself from the object of his prizing; (2) the nature of the being that is believed: it is a person or idea that cannot be recognized except through a nonpossessive recognition; (3) and the nature of the relation between believer and believed: it is a relation that enlarges the believer. In this complex reality we meet not only the profoundly ethical character of the relation between ourselves and other persons, between our minds and the ideas that govern them; we meet also with the moral nature of our most essential being. Believing is not merely a means but it is also a medium of our existence; it is of the very matter of our being. It is the integument of our life with others, the energy by which we hold fast to

12. The threat of the collapse of prophecy (and hence of faith) appears in Jeremiah's protest to God that he has deceived his prophet. The deceitfulness of God is a possibility that even natural science fears. "Raffiniert ist der Herr Gott aber nicht böse," Einstein is reported to have said. Philosophy today only discusses the existence or nonexistence of God, his goodness or his limitedness; it does not entertain the notion of his possible deceitfulness. Jesus' word from the cross, "My God, my God, why hast thou forsaken me?" has planted deep in Christian faith the suspicion that Jeremiah first raised overtly, and so it has intensified faith as believing to its highest possible pitch of self-consciousness, by making such faith a struggle with the temptation to disbelieve the constancy of God. After Jeremiah and Jesus, the faith they symbolize can never again be a matter of course.

13. See "Essay on Faith," *The Works of S. T. Coleridge*, vol. 5.

principles, the giver of whatever confidence we have in ourselves. When we understand believing in this manner, as a spécific human way of taking hold of the agent-world and sharing in its power, we have a clearer notion of moral agency and power in our own human existence, of our own personal "substantiality." Believing reveals human being as that which seeks other being, as that which tends to enlarge its world and itself, not only by greater and clearer knowledge or by consumption and annexation of property but by the peculiar conduct of holding dear.[14] In this way believing enters into the forming of persons.

IV. Believing and Isolation

Although believing is a native strength of ours in this field of powers, we recognize the limited scope of its effectiveness in our lives. If we think of adulthood as a taking charge of ourselves, then we recognize that we are reluctant people, more like adolescents fitfully growing and asserting ourselves, now in this direction, now in that. We do not dare to know ourselves. We recognize that restrictive images rule our moral imagination. While we are making ourselves one with humankind in our body, the earth, we do not make ourselves equally generous in our attitudes and actions toward other peoples. The effect is that our generosity paradoxically dwindles as it grows. We also recognize the incongruity between our confidence in nature and our lack of confidence in ourselves. Each day we taste the sands of erosion. Some of this recognition betrays itself in our nostalgia for a pastoral life, for an earlier age of faith or of simplicity, for a medieval synthesis of belief and science, for a Reformation ardor of faith transforming church, nation, and university—in

14. The view of human believing as both a mode of awareness involving admiration and a mode of human being leads to the conclusion that statements of belief (the expressions of believing) are not simple descriptions of some reality but are part of the reference to which they themselves refer. Such statements are actualizations of the being from which they come and to which they refer, and in being made they change the world to which they belong. See below in this chapter, sec. V.

a word, for some lost Christendom. Of course, we exaggerate the unity and vigor of this Christendom gone by. Nostalgia for times past tricks us into perceiving a greater unity in them than was there. In part this illusion is due to our present feeling of distractedness.[15] Even so, the notion of a bygone Christendom illustrates our instinctive appreciation of the power of synchronous believing to assist in the shaping of a world and to give directedness and identity to the individual.

By contrast with these idealized lost ages the present displays little apparent harmony. The environing field of powers is a protean field, in which many worlds are latent. It shows now this shape and character and now that, according to the kind of human interest that makes the axis of our interaction with it. When the scientific interest predominates, for example, the field of time and space begins to clarify into a world of predictions. It takes on the semblance of the left-hand member of an equation for which there is a proportional answer. This clarity, however, is the clarity of relations between classes of events and of beings; it is not clarity of the thicket of our experience.

In any case, we can rarely indulge scientific interests for their own sake. Our political nature must assert itself, and when political interests do press forward, the scene alters. The political world cannot be construed as a set of problems and answers. It is a more pressing world, demanding action of men before they can comprehend it. It displays a denser, more urgent and ominous unity.

And when the axis of the relation to the environment is religion and faith, another change overcomes us. The scientific intelligibility of the world recedes ever further, for now the individual's interest moves him toward the thicket of experience as a whole. He asks: What kind of power governs the field of these powers? What strength do I require to engage in and with

15. "Nostalgia for other people's lives. This is because, seen from the outside, they form a whole, while our life, seen from the inside, is all bits and pieces. Once again, we run after an illusion of unity." Albert Camus, *Carnets 1942-1951*, trans. P. Thody, London (1966), 17.

this kinetic field? There is nothing, however, with which the inquiring man can compare this undefined totality except the one thing given immediately to him, his own life. Yet his life is part of the field of powers making up his world. Therefore, while the interest of faith in the opposing field of powers carries the most intense sense of the unity of the world, it is least capable of reducing the world to the intelligibility that takes the form of question and answer.[16] The faith-interest instead strives to reproduce the unity of the encompassing field of powers in the unity of the individual's life, and conversely to discover the unity of individual life in the opposing world. Consequently, the religious interest in our world as a whole draws us again into exploration of all the ways in which we conduct ourselves in the field of our existence as we search for analogies that will suggest the nature of our destiny.

This environment with its latency of many communities of believing and many worlds has been coming into existence for decades. Now that it is here, life is a repetition of births, in which our earlier bodies of experience are never quite sloughed off and our former passions and worlds never entirely transfigured. Birth into the family is only the first, followed by births into schools, universities, and economic markets, into citizenship and its cares, war, the professional guild or union, and the laboratory. With each birth the "tides of faith" recede from the individual. The energy of believing that shaped his former world does not affect his new companions. The university's moral energy, for example, appears so differently from the family's. And those who formerly were inwardly alike and stood toward each other as communicants of shared moral strengths and intellectual virtues, in family, church, or school, now feel themselves to be stranded in separated spaces. So the university student or Vietnam veteran looking back sees an irremedial distance between his family and himself. As these births and strandings occur, men suffer not simply because familiar beliefs and dogmas

16. The question-answer form is the most inappropriate for theology.

ebb away, but also because their new world has less of familiar virture evident in it, specifically less recognized expenditure of the moral energy of believing and hence less substance. On the one hand, the field of human interaction as it becomes ever broader and more indistinct leaves men isolated and impervious, less easily touched by the believing of other men. Their minds subside toward the equilibrium of indifference. On the other hand, the polymorphous capability of the man-age creates an expanding vista of possible forms of action and human intercourse: worlds possible in which the individual sees men at work or in conversation animated by some mysterious seriousness and gladness of which he himself, however, has yet no part. And the mind, consequently, is oppressed by bewilderment and yearning toward these desirable but remote societies.[17]

In the polymorphous present age, radial man knows many interests and passions. None masters him by nature. Many super-

17. These states are reflected in the following personal utterances: "I am where my feet lay watching the roads, the endless roads, the infinite number of roads . . . . My mind is the conspirator to the ends, the infinite ends. It follows each path anew yearning and despairing . . . . Or, or, or is it energy which starts these paths, and do they continue, do they continue unseen by me? Are they covered by the fullness of the hills? Are they low on the ground and lost in the hilly landscape? And the mountains, the mountains which are formed by the roads, the mountains which are the roads, roads lost. Can a road form a barrier to another road? The mountains which are the roads form plains. High, rocky and inhuman, yet they are plains . . . plains of many colors and of many roads.—The people are in the sea and the sea forms stones, separates the land. As do too many roads which cross each other." H. Westman, *The Springs of Creativity*, London (1961), 240 ("The Case of Joan").

"But upon a day, the good providence of God did cast me to *Bedford*, to work on my calling; and in one of the streets of that town, I came where there was three or four poor women sitting at a door in the Sun, and talking about the things of God; and being now willing to hear them discourse, I drew near to hear what they said; for I was now a brisk talker also myself in the matters of Religion: but now I may say, *I heard, but I understood not;* for they were far above my reach . . . . And me thought they spoke as if joy did make them speak: they spake with such pleasantness of Scripture language, and with such appearance of grace in all they said, that they were to me as if they had found a new world, as they were people that dwelt alone, and were not to be reckoned among their Neighbours. Num. 23.9.— At this I felt my own heart began to shake, as mistrusting my condition to be naught." John Bunyan, *Grace Abounding to the Chief of Sinners*, pars. 37, 38, 39.

personalities and institutions polarize his world. None has the power, either attractive or coercive, to shape it as a whole. Hence, he lives "in and out" of many nascent worlds. In none is he at home. The "giddiness" that thereby overcomes him awakens him to frustration and disenchantment, also to adventure and discovery.[18] Therefore, the already formed beliefs of the Christian society do not suffice to express the believing energy of such a man of many origins. For believing is not commanded by beliefs. Beliefs come from believing; and believing is generated in experience. Believing finds satisfaction only in such statements as both express and enhance the whole scope and intensity of the experience from which it arises and to which it must contribute. The traditional beliefs of the Christian society (its dogma of Christ's two natures, its definitions of the grace in the sacraments, or its doctrine of the providence of God) appear increasingly as beliefs that fail to augment the strength of the man who must find the moral and intellectual energy to reconcile the many birthplaces and societies he carries in himself. They appear increasingly to attract doubting rather than believing.

18. The recognition of this situation of inner and outer manyness is part of the motive for the theology which calls attention to (and takes its name from) the phenomenon of "secular Christianity." The very presence of such a theology—urging Christians to let go their image of themselves as church dwellers—is as symptomatic of this age of plural worlds as the other features in our culture that are so striking: nonfiction novels, "camera-eye" reportage, and the many other evidences of hunger for and obsession by immediate, personal experience. What these phenomena manifest is that the multiple human worlds, in which even the Christianly self-conscious person lives, extend far beyond the boundaries of any established institution.

The turn toward the "secular gospel" is the mark of a generation which grew up in a time when theologians were making the church the center of Christian believing and defending Christian doctrine on the grounds that it articulated church experience rather than general human experience, or experience born of the Word of God rather than experience expressible in human words. The theology that was ecclesio-centered thus produced its own antithesis: secular Christianity. Both kinds of theology lack insight into the fact that the experience from which believing arises is neither ecclesiastical, nor biblical, nor secular. It is simply human or experience of the times.

V. Believing and Doubting

Nevertheless, the evident disparity between the particular beliefs the Christian society has conserved and the experiential worlds of human beings in this age is not the simple opposition between believing, on the one hand, and doubting, on the other. It is rather a disparity between the withered strength of a belief or set of beliefs adrift, severed from its matrix, and the burgeoning life of the human world in which it lingers. The mental action of doubting is an action that diverts the energy of believing from its accustomed channels or directs it away from its habitual symbols. Thus, doubting may separate a belief from believing, but it is not a negation of believing as such. It is itself a particular way of managing the energy of believing.

The yoke of doubting and believing is illustrated in the history and present circumstances of the old Christian belief and doctrine that God is a providing-God. For the belief that God is a providing-God, a governing-God, is a doctrine that believing experience has generated several times in the history of Jewish and Christian culture, from the exile of Israel in Babylon to the settlement of the Amercan wilderness by the English Puritans and Separatists. Now, however, this belief attracts to itself a massive doubting that encysts it in the modern mind and isolates it as a foreign body from the past. Yet such rejection of alien belief is part of striving in a believing way with present human experience.

Whenever we are able to observe the doctrine of providence or of the providing-God in its actual genesis, in the prophecies of II Isaiah, or in Jesus' parables of the Kingdom, in Augustine's *Confessions*, in Calvin's chapters on providence in *The Institutes of the Christian Religion*, or in Jonathan Edwards' sermons on the *History of the Work of Redemption*, we see that the intention and function of the belief itself is to represent and symbolize the way in which these men hold dear or believingly organize the entire field of their experience. The "providing-God," as a living symbol, is an "outering" of the believing that belongs to the endeavor to make a judgment about the tendency of the agent-world as a whole and of human being in that world. The profession that God governs the course of human affairs for good is a judgment which puts together the hazards and fortuitous moments of life in the street, life constantly intensified and stretched out in surprising and dismaying events, and affirms that this whole of experience—incomplete, asymmetrical, and often dissonant—is good. It is good not "on balance" or despite the evil in it, but good because it is the vehicle of God's intentions. This is, moreover, for the believing man the only real goodness that he can lay hold on in experience.

One need only read the parables of the Kingdom, the *Confessions* of Augustine, or the *Institutes* to see that these believers do not attempt to find proportion, symmetry of relation, compensation, or balance within the field of their experience, within their own lives or the lives of others. "Providence" is not an answer to Jesus' question: Why did the tower fall on these men? Nor does it prevent Augustine's protesting prayer: "How much better had it been for me to have been speedily cured. . . ."[19] If anything, as "doctrine" providence sets aside visibility of pattern and symmetry within personal experience.[20] When, therefore, a man wrestles with the unlikeness of today to yesterday, with the randomness and disparateness of the elements of his own life-course and ambience, and then looks to the doctrine of providence for

19. *Confessions*, I, xi.
20. A deep misunderstanding of believing and belief, in religious faith, informs the criticisms of contemporary philosophers in the analytical tradition, who doubt the meaningfulness of Christian or "theistic" beliefs because they do not provide answers to questions of fact. Beliefs are not intended as the answers to questions of fact but as the expressions of judgments about the field of experience as such. Nevertheless, the dialectical form that theology has so often assumed, from Anselm to Tillich, encourages this misconception.

Wittgenstein comes closer to the truth of the nature of statements setting out our believing when he remarks: "Ethics does not treat of the world. Ethics must be a condition of the world (viz. Life [*sic*]), like logic." The context of this observation indicates that the author was thinking similarly about religious faith and theology. See *Notebooks: 1914-1916*, trans. G. E. M. Anscombe, New York (1961), 77[e].

a method of eliciting clarity, balance, and equity where otherwise they do not appear, he can only end by doubting the meaning of the belief itself. He doubts the belief of a providing-God, because the providence for which he looks and which he does not find is a providential ordering of his own history. But, in the mind of Jesus or Augustine, believing in God-providing expresses confidence in an order not in the history of the self but in the works of God, an order not within the time of the individual's birth and death but an infinite order, to which the birth, life, and death of the individual belong. Therefore, the misinterpreted doctrine of providence has no power of associating ideas or of organizing images to render harmony and unity among the energies soliciting and attacking man in this radial age.[21] It could become significant, only if the man who suffers in this manyness both inwardly and outwardly were to ask: To what use is my incomplete human existence in such a radial world being put? And in response to this kind of question, only judgments that become consciously believing judgments concerning the whole world—judgments approving and disapproving—can supply a commensurate symbolic statement that represents the scope of experience from which the question arises.[22]

When, for example, men perceive that the life of Jesus of Nazareth—as full as any life can be and also as fragmented and lacking in Emersonian symmetry and compensation as any life can—elicits from themselves the judgment, It is good! they find

21. The misunderstanding of providence, and by extension, election, as doctrines of manifest patterns of equity, recompense, proportion, etc., in personal and national history is evident especially among existentialists today. Rudolf Bultmann, for example, takes the contingency-character of human history as a barrier to belief, because the contingent exhibits no divine government. And Sartre supposes that the doctrine of election means inwardly heard mandates and directives from God. In a word, providence and election stand in opposition to the openness of personal history, in the mind of the existentialist, while in the mind of the prophet, of Augustine, etc., providence and election are expressions of the convictions that just this openness and incompleteness is meaningful. These doctrines say, not that history is God's masterpiece, but that it is his material.

22. The matter can be put this way. Only when the individual uses his mythic or faith-imagination, as well as his scientific imagination, will he understand the function of religious symbols.

that statements about this messiah-prophet-servant become for them symbols expressing and reacting upon their own believing experience of their own incomplete lives and of their nieghbors' lives and of their agent-world as a whole.

Still, men and women in this age enjoy such perceptions only rarely, when their own experience coincides in this way with that of the prophets and saints. So that around the belief of a providing-God it is doubting that abounds, not believing. The same is evident of many another belief that Christian and christianized societies conserve but do not generate in experience.

Yet since doubting draws on the same mental and moral energy as believing, the prevalence of doubt concerning specific beliefs is not a sign of the absence of this energy but rather of the fact that it is following different directions and issuing through different kinds of experience. Indeed, the paramountcy of believing and human beliefulness is, if anything, more striking in the present world/age than is our evidence of it in any other, including the so-called age of belief. For the citizen of the radial world lives daily in its midst and finds his life to be a continuing contest with it. In the reading of newspapers, the watching of television on-the-scene-reportage and documentaries, and the ingestion of unending news comment and analysis, he employs and seeks to train the passion of believing into a virtue. In the global operations of the great news-gathering organizations, we are able to see how human beliefulness has become a chief moral energy of the human world, giving it its coherence. Because each of us today is asked to hear, to see, to suffer more of the words and images of other men as vehicles of their passions, he is also asked to believe more. A member of our present generations expends an unmeasured fund of psychic energy in taking on credence or in rejecting what others pass on to him through the telecommunications system of our earth. His ability to make judgments and so to understand what is happening to him in his earth-body is founded upon the repertorial and editorial staffs of the great mass media, upon the intelligence agencies of governments, upon the expert learnedness of Chinese or Russian or

South American specialists in universities and state departments, upon the predictive and interpretative skills of medical scholars and professional observers of the behavior of money. And these agencies of collection and analysis of information, from which come judgments about the import and direction of human affairs as a whole, are themselves corporate bodies of human intelligence and beliefulness, displaying their own attitudes toward the world of power and their own methods of taking hold of that power and paying deference to it. In short, these agencies show personas or ways of faith which we must either trust or distrust but of which we cannot be independent. They demonstrate the fact that the more important is our individual and general public intelligence regarding this great world of action, the more each of us is called upon to manage the human energy of believing.[23]

When an eminent historian, famous after years of service in the White House, says that he will never again trust newspaper

23. Newspaper accounts are statements representing the judgments of others, which the reader must accept, modify, or discredit, as he thinks fit. The activity of the newspaper reader is, in essence, no different from that of the reader of a scientific journal or of a history book. The differences between these two readers have to do not with their subject matter but with the leisure at their disposal for the inspection and criticism of the judgments put before them and the amount of expertness they bring to the work of directing their belief. (But a man may be, of course, an expert reader of newspapers, as was the late A. J. Liebling who reported on them for many years in *The New Yorker.*) The modern newspaper illustrates the fact that the individual has no option today but to be a vessel of the moral energy of belief, if he is conscious of the position of man on and in the earth.

The photograph plays an equal if not greater role in reportorial and editorial communication. Whether it be cinematic or still photography is beside the point here. The pertinent fact is that—as the word itself tells us —men write or draw with light what they have seen and wish others to see. The viewer of the photograph must direct his believing toward or away from the photographer. Since most published photographs are anonymous, this process of directing believing tends to become nearly unconscious or automatic on our part, but we are believers nevertheless, whenever we look at and into a photograph. The contention that photographs are simply reproductions of reality and hence require no belief has no force for two reasons: (1) the camera and darkroom are as much instruments of the agent as the chisel or palette; (2) "reproductions of reality" must be believed to be reproductions of reality.

accounts of political events, he only underlines thereby the fact that the expenditure of beliefulness can never be stopped or dammed up but only served with fidelity or corrupted. Hence, our peculiar twentieth-century awareness of the depths of human deceitfulness —our credibility gaps—is also an awareness of the ever-mounting importance of the critical role beliefulness plays in our lives. When men are stripped of the power of believing, they are helpless in the turmoil of their own experience, calmed by no common spirit of wholeness.

* * *

So a species of confiding appears to be ingredient in all enterprises requiring the sharing of observation, thinking, and knowing. Confidence, conscience, and cooperation are coeval virtues in human nature. The energy of believing is something common of all men. Beliefulness is a kind of faithfulness that the passion of the inquiring and judging mind brings to birth in all. Yet the field of our generations' experiences is a great field, latent with multiple human worlds for each individual. No single society or institution in that field can be the chief custodian of human believing. Though if none was willing to conserve, be it as chief or simply humble custodian, we would lose our history as believing men. Nevertheless, the beliefs which the Christian church conserves have no intrinsic authority, as church beliefs, to compel the citizen of the radial world to enter into them. He need not and cannot share beliefs without also sharing the believing that engendered them, and he cannot share the believing that engendered them, unless he also shares the experience of which such believing is a part. Only in such geneses do men learn that they must hold dear what is not and cannot be their own possession.

Nevertheless, the moral energy of believing is fundamental, quite irrespective of the primacy of church, giving much of what beauty, coherence, and directedness there is in our human world. A man acquires his persona in his action of believing. While many men today may lack the qualities of sacramental faith or Reformation ardor, we may still call these times an age in which the exercise and admiration of human beliefulness is unmistakable and preeminent. This is a generation as much dependent on the unquenchable sources of such believing as men have ever been. Consequently, we look beyond the powerlessness of the too stylized and contracted beliefs of institutional Christendom to the experience itself from which believing arises. And we ask whether there is a belief-generating experience that men share, just as they share in the necessity of directing the moral energy of beliefulness, simply because they have their being in a common human world.

The answer that the following chapter elaborates is that there is a shared experience that generates in men an awareness of themselves as believing beings, as persons who hold dear. It is the experience in which the affectional "stuff" of human faithfulness most directly appears: the experience of diminution and of gladness.

chapter 4
Fear and Gladness

Believing belongs to experience. It does not generate itself. It arises in the times of testing in which human faithfulness takes shape and becomes tangible as an affection. Our business now is to look at these experiences, or testings, in which faith appears as affectional.

I. Recapitulation

Of course, human faith is more than an affection. But its affective character is the one stratum among the several we know in ourselves that we most neglect to describe, understand, and interpret. If we choose the single metaphor of awakening for this complex reality, faith, then we may put the whole matter in the following ways: We awaken to our own existence, as Descartes long ago taught, when we come to perceive that we are thinking beings. *Cogito ergo sum.* Here is a fundament of certitude. We find ourselves engaged with a world eliciting the mind's activity of reasoning. And as thinking beings who are also moved by the ancient springs of religion, we respond by seeking an understanding of the world commensurate with our religious striving for alinement with true power.

Again, we awaken to our existence in the experience of taking responsibility for our lives, in acts of willing, of resolving, and of doubting. *Ago ergo sum. Volo ergo sum. Dubito ergo sum.* Here is another certitude: the agency that is me and us. And our whole world appears to us a world demanding of us enterprise and courage. As willing and doubting and asserting beings we respond in our religious striving through actions of willing, through decisions to discard old ways, and through risks of confidence beyond the range of visible evidences.

But in addition we awaken to our being in suffering and being acted upon. *Patior ergo sum.* This is the original and encompassing experience that gives its form to all particular experiences, for neither thinking nor willing and acting on the environment are appropriate or conceivable human responses unless the field of surrounding forces disposes men toward thought and action in that field. Suffering then is also a boundary of existence, an ever-present element of consciousness, and correspondingly our world appears to us a field of energies converging on us, shaping us, distending us, shattering us, and sending us on paths we have not chosen for ourselves.

The suffering of which we are thinking here is not simply consciousness of pain, grief, and limitation, although these things belong to daily living. The suffering before us now is a determinant of all experience, whatever its specific kind. It appears, for example, in the inability of a man to add "a cubit to his stature," in the chance character of the world that awards unequal labor with equal profit, in the surprisingness of the world that yields a find of great value to a man who is not even looking. The metaphysical name that some have given this characteristic of human existence is finitude, but the experiential matter itself is suffering, the pathos that stands in opposition and correlation to the enworlding field of power.

Suffering of this order as something universal is the matrix that generates the passion of believing. It is the medium in which faithfulness forms and appears in determinate shapes in our radial world. In order to understand how this is so, we need to bring together in our minds three features of faithfulness within the horizon of suffering. We have already attended to the first in chapter 2 and need only recall it here. We have alluded to the second, also in chapter 2 (sec. III), and will briefly examine it again. Then, to the third we will devote the body of this chapter.

The first is the equivalence of faithfulness to nothing less than a man's whole conduct, both his outer way of sharing in his physical and social world and his inner conduct toward himself. The very particular and momentary appearances of faith as a rational action of assenting to a statement, such as the profession that God is all-powerful, or as an action of deciding, such as choosing a policy, belong to this more comprehensive reality, namely, to a man's self-government among the energies that surround him and well up within him as his vitality. We may say in the language of western antiquity that faith is a man's persona, his method of sharing in the economy of his age. It is his disposition as a whole, or—more commonly—it is his several dispositions, so that we more accurately speak of a man's faiths than of his faith and of his personas than of his one persona. Faith-fulness appears as the manner in which human being comports itself within its world of power. If we now put the same matter into our present language of suffering, then we affirm that a man's faith-fulness is the way in which he accepts and addresses himself to his situation as a suffering being.

The second feature of human faith-fulness within the horizon of suffering is the fact that it does not arise in any man utterly afresh. We recall, for example, the relation we found to exist between human religion and human faith. The fact that each always seems to appear as the background for the other indicates that in experience of this kind we come across no absolute beginnings. Therefore, in the special ways that men are tested in this age, the radial world of our modern mythic figure radial man, such faithfulness as we find shows itself only as springing from a soil seeded by earlier religion and faith, so that each new appearance of human faithfulness rises before us as a mutation of that which has gone before.

The experience of faith is in this respect analogous to that of thinking. When Descartes awakened in the experience of thinking to the firm, indubitable reality of his own rational being, that awakening was more than the awakening of the individual, Descartes. With and in his discovery there awakened again the Platonism of the foregoing centuries together with the long warfare between the followers of Aristotle and Plato.

History gives us scarcely an instance of thought beginning absolutely afresh but rather instances of thought arising anew in forms that were hitherto inhibited and hidden by other great regulating tenets and ideas. The situation in which men awaken to suffering and faith is similar. On the one hand, to exist faithfully is to exist in one's own experience. It is to awaken in such and such a way to a world that is pressing in. We may say (in more technical language) that faith is something propriate. It belongs to the individual person. Faith is a man's persona. Hence, just as your awakening cannot be my awakening; nor your taste of bitterness mine; so your faith cannot be mine nor mine yours. Yet, on the other hand, whoever suffers in this peculiar manner we call human faith awakens to a world in which many faith-experiences have already flourished and died, while others are just coming into being. Therefore, in each man's awakening echo the awakenings of other men, of other generations, and of other societies. When one reads Thomas Aquinas' descriptions of faith as an inchoate intellectual vision of God and as assent to the teachings of the church about God, it is apparent that the faith he knew best for himself is one that resounds with the affirmations of many men who awakened before him to the God who is universal Logos shaping the world by the creative goodness of his own simplicity. When Calvin called faith a firm knowledge of God's benevolence, sealed in the heart, his affirmation recalled and was amplified by the sense of a burning heart in many a man before him, in Jeremiah, in the disciples on the Emmaus road, in Augustine. When Jonathan Edwards confessed to a new taste and perception of the beauty and excellence of Christ, of God, and of nature, his confession evoked and justified afresh all those from Moses to Isaiah to the seventeenth-century mystics whose faith was a new perception of the beauty and holiness, the glory of God.

This resonance of past testimonies in the present awakening of a man, this resurrection of earlier worlds in the present radial world of suffering, implies, however, that dissonance also characterizes the experience of faith. There is dissonance between the broadly Platonic experience-world of the Fourth Gospel and the dynamic, apocalyptic world of Mark, for example. There is dissonance between the ordered, soaring, crystalline world of Aquinas and the enigmatic world of Calvin. There is a harsh incompatibility between the Sysiphus experience of the existentialist and the perfectedness, completeness of the world of Leibniz. To awaken in resonance with one of these means to stand in conflict with the other. To live in and employ the symbols of one of these experience-worlds is to perceive the symbols of the other as shallow, opaque, and distorted. The experience of faith carries within itself, therefore, not only the sense of awakening, of new-mindedness, of new engagement with a new world, but also the experience of conflict and strife. The consequence is that there is always, for the faithful man, some other human world sounding with testimonies to which he himself cannot give voice, some other world of faithfulness that appears to him as dead and hollow or—at worst—demonic. To awaken is to become contemporary with other men whose thoughts, actions, and way of life appear as stifled and obscure and yet as real.

From the understanding of this complex and antithetical situation of awakening there follows a very practical consequence for our further understanding of the geneses of human faith. No individual, be he child or man, ever enters into a new mind alone. He enters in company with earlier authors of that quality of new-mindedness and also in company with those who oppose its peculiar qualities. The individual, to whatever age he belongs, does not stand in simple innocence, as it were, before the "pioneer and perfecter of his faith" be it Abraham, or Moses, or Jesus of Nazareth, or Socrates. He stands as a man in whom the vestiges and echoes of many other partly harmonizing, partly conflicting confessions make themselves known. He is half-blinded by the sclerotic residues of past religion and faith in his own man-age. He is shaped and invaded by the alien experiences of other men surrounding him. Yet no world of faith can come alive for him without such "negative" determinants being present in some way. So far as the post-Christian or the would-be Christian or *homo Christianus*[1] is concerned, the ultimate authorizer of his faith, Jesus of Nazareth, never comes alive for him as a solitary figure but only as part of an experience-world in which there are negative as well as harmonizing voices testifying to him. For this man, even in his new-mindedness, deadening as well as living symbols always surround the Christ he meets in worship, in reading the New Testament, in watching the motion picture or the drama of the Christ figure.

When, therefore, we ask about the geneses of Christ-patterned faith, whether for the first or the seventieth time, in *homo Christianus*, and about the marks that set such faith off from the general background of human religion and faithfulness, we can receive no helpful answer so long as we look for what does not exist and focus our attention on what cannot be seen: a pure image of the ultimate authority of true human faithfulness. The captain and perfecter of Christian faith remains hemmed in by crowds of our predecessors and aloof from our scientific demand in this historical and social confusion. Clarity does not reach us from a source that is itself not clear to perception shaped in a human world marred by dissonance and conflict. All of the dogmatic labors a theologian may devote to the definition of Christ, all of the research that a historian may expend in the search for the historical Jesus, by whatever methods he may

1. For the meaning we attach to this term, see chap. 1, p. 9, note.

devise, will fail to create clarity in the figure of Jesus—until we understand what it is in our world/age that endows our own experience with resonance to the world of Jesus and that enables us to recognize his conduct and his method of taking hold of the known and paying deference to the unknown as authoritative, augmenting, and attractive to us in our enigmatic world.

Therefore our question is now: What kind of experience is greater than, and surmounts the conflict of, testimonies and interests? What makes believing a "natural" relation to the person about whose definition men contend? What kind of awakening to world and faithfulness creates in radial man the apperceptive mass to single out Jesus in the confused background of his and our social history as a distinctive authority? Our initial query is not: What gives Jesus clarity? It is: What gives him importance in a radial world? We may put the question again in this way. Where do men make a beginning in their own experience of faith in this power-world that they may recognize the new beginning that Christ himself represents and embodies? For the biblical figure of Jesus is insignificant (and irrelevant to the theological and ideological disputes surrounding him), apart from a converging of our perception of him in his world and our perception of ourselves in our world:

The answer that we make is that the beginning lies in the experience of faith that is affectional: in enigmatic suffering of the world of power. But in order to see how this is so, we must attend to the third feature of faith within the horizon of suffering: to the double experience of being diminished and being enlarged, experiences that run throughout the sayings of Jesus as he spoke of the ruling action of God and that we meet in the affections of fear and gladness.

II. Fearing

Religious man as a fearing being is familiar to us directly and through a quantity of literature about dread, melancholy, and anxiety, beginning at least with Aristotle. He is man subject to "fear of things not fearful" and man confessing that "fear of death disorders me."

In order to follow this subject, however, we have to acknowledge an issue posed by the current usage of terms for fear. For in recent literature, particularly since the rise of Kierkegaard's influence, theological and philosophical students of the soul have distinguished between fear and dread, reserving the terms dread and anxiety as the names for the state of mind in which a man is fearful yet has no object of fear before him; while they have used the word fear for the emotions of repulsion, fright, and so forth in the face of particular threats and powers. This distinction is, without doubt, a valuable one, helping us to sharpen our perception of human existence in our world and to recognize that trembling comes on us often for no namable reason. It is, however, by no means the only significant distinction to be made in this area of inquiry and description. Moreover, the distinction itself, once it has been made, enables us to see that the experience it is designed to illuminate is ambiguous. Our responses of fright and flight in the face of particular inimical powers often draw their momentum as much from the dreading or fearing state of mind as they do from the seemingly harmful objects themselves. But rarely, if ever, does our experience itself show us wholly object-less dreading or purely objective fearing. The distinction is, consequently, theoretical, and its value lies in calling our attention to the doubleness of such states of mind, not the separateness of "fear" and "dread."

There is, furthermore, nothing in the history of the terms fear, anxiety, dread, to warrant the use of the first for the strictly object-induced, individual passionate reactions of the mind and the latter for the general condition alone. The convention that Kierkegaard and the philosopher Heidegger have introduced is a somewhat arbitrary one. While on the contrary, there is much to be said for speaking simply of fear with its dual and ambiguous nature. For fear remains the most flexible and generic word and in its history shares the connotation that is most important for our purposes, namely, the sensation of hesitation and withdrawal from the dangers that attend all travel, all movement in and through time, that attend every moment of "passing or going through," that is to say, that attend all *experience*.[2]

In what follows we shall use dread and fear indifferently, meaning the same states by these two words (and also by anxiety), leaving it to the context to signify our intention of emphasizing the particular or the general aspect of fearing.

Kierkegaard—to resume—is for most of us the modern prophet

2. The English fear is associated with the German *Gefahr* and *fahren*, the Latin *experior*, and the Greek *poros*. A pair of examples from Englishmen, in which both fear and dread appear for similar states of mind, illustrates the inconvenience of attempting to reserve those words for quite distinct conditions. The first is taken from a letter written by John Donne: "I observe the physician with the same diligence as he the disease. I see he fears, and I fear with him. I overtake him. I overrun him in his fear, because he makes his pace slow; I fear the more, because he disguises his fear, and I see it with the more sharpness because he would not have me see it . . . . I fear not the hastening of my death, and yet I do fear the increase of the disease." *The Life and Letters of John Donne*, ed. Edmund Gosse, London (1899), vol. 2, 184.

The other example is S. T. Coleridge's, in his notebooks: "It is a most instructive part of my Life the fact, that I have been always preyed on by some Dread, and perhaps all my faulty actions have been the consequence of some Dread or other on my mind / from fear of Pain, of Shame, not from prospect of Pleasure / —So in my childhood and Boyhood the horror of being detected with a sorehead; afterwards imaginary fears of . . . having the Itch in my Blood— / then a short-lived Fit of Fears from sex—then horror of Duns, and a state of struggling with madness from an incapability of hoping that I should be able to marry Mary Evans (and this strange passion of fervent tho' wholly imaginative and imaginary Love uncombinable by my utmost efforts with ⟨any regular⟩ Hope— / possibly from deficiency of bodily feeling, of tactual ideas connected with the image) had all the effects of direct Fear, and I have lain for hours together awake at night, groaning and praying—Then came that stormy time / and for a few months America really inspired Hope, and I became an exalted Being—then came Rob. Southey's alienation / my marriage—constant dread in my mind respecting Mrs. Coleridge's Temper, &c—and finally stimulants in the fear and prevention of violent Bowel-attacks from mental agitation / then ⟨almost epileptic⟩ night-horrors in my sleep / and since then every error I have committed, has been the immediate effect of the Dread of these bad most shocking Dreams—any thing to prevent them / —all this interwoven with its minor consequences, that fill up the interspaces—the cherry juice running in between the cherries in a cherry pie / procrastination in dread of this— and something else in consequence of that procrast. &c—and from the same cause the least languor expressed in a Letter from S.H. drives me wild / and it is most unfortunate that I so fearfully despondent should have concentered my soul thus on one almost as feeble in Hope as myself. 11 Jan. 1805." *The Notebooks of Samuel Taylor Coleridge*, ed. Kathleen Coburn, vol. 2, New York (1961), no. 2398.

of the religious and Christian meanings of the affection of dread, and his book *The Concept of Dread* has been the stimulus for much of twentieth-century theological and philosophical reflection on the tonalities of our existence. According to Kierkegaard, dread is a "qualification of the dreaming spirit"; it is the name of the peculiar psychic weight that oppresses the solitary individual as he becomes aware of the freedom he cannot put aside. It is the affective condition in which the untried, innocent spirit is both attracted to, and repelled from, any and every specific possible choice and commitment that it might make. Dread also, in the role of objective or socially amplified and contagious dread, overwhelms the individual, insofar as he is not only a unique agent but a member of the race, and corrupts him by its all-pervading, alienating power.

Valuable as Kierkegaard's psychological essay into anxiety may be, however, it is inadequate; partly because Kierkegaard himself was one of those Romantics who relished melancholy, a subspecies of fear, as a sign of genius;[3] partly because he failed to set dread in the full context in which it actually appears, in the dynamic field of human existence in the world of power. Kierkegaard recognized the theoretical importance of "objective dread," but he gave it only formal recognition and little room in his skillful portrayals of dreading human beings. We need, therefore, to supplement Kierkegaard, and it will be better if we do so by looking to direct and personal expressions of fearing rather than simply to literary, philosophical, and theological

3. Kierkegaard wrote as follows about his melancholy: "In addition to the wide circle of my acquaintances with whom I am, on the whole, on a very formal footing, I still have an intimate, confidential friend—my melancholy, and in the midst of my pleasure, in the midst of my work, she beckons me, calls me aside, even though physically I remain where I am, she is the most faithful mistress I have known. But what wonder then that I must be ready to follow her at any moment of the day." *Journals of Søren Kierkegaard*, trans. A. Dru, Oxford (1951), no. 359. For a discussion of the Romantic idea of melancholy as a sign of genius, see Klibansky, *et al.*, *Saturn and Melancholy*. Note here the place that Kant occupies in the history of the discussion of melancholy. "The 'sadness without cause'" indicated "possession of a moral scale which destroyed personal happiness by the merciless revelation of his own and others' worthlessness" (122).

reflections on it. The pages of diaries, journals, autobiographies, and notebooks are full of examples.

One that is obviously dated as a literary item but distinctive and typical of the phenomenon otherwise is in the journals of David Brainerd, dated "Lord's Day, August 5," 1744:

Towards night was extremely weak, faint, sick, and full of pain . . . . I am obliged to let all my thoughts and concerns run at random; for I have not strength to read, meditate, or pray: and this naturally perplexes my mind. I seem to myself like a man that has all his estate embarked in one small boat, unhappily going adrift, down a swift torrent. The poor owner stands on the shore, and looks, and laments his loss—But, alas! though my all seems to be adrift, and I stand and see it, I dare not lament; for this sinks my spirits more, and aggravates my bodily disorders! I am forced therefore to divert myself with trifles; although at the same time I am afraid, and often feel as if I was guilty of the misimprovement of time.[4]

Brainerd's complaint virtually interprets itself, for it shows nearly all of the classic features of the fearing, dreading state of mind, in which no particular element or object sufficiently threatens the self to account for the condition, yet the entire self-world polarity resounds with the affection. These are clearly the words of a man—however foreign his piety may seem to the reader—who is the subject of the experience of diminution. In addition to the striking imagery employed (which is repeated in other, diverse and equally spontaneous exclamations of despair[5]), one of the features that makes this example typical is the fact that Brainerd's picture of himself is that of a man who knows that if he admits he is in dread, his dreading will grow more powerful. Self-understanding here offers no antidote. Therefore, although the language is not only eighteenth-century American but peculiar to the unusual David Brainerd, this self-examination of a lonely spirit in the American wilderness represents accurately

4. *Memoirs of the Rev. David Brainerd*, 160.
5. W. H. Auden has investigated the literary symbolism of despair, sea, water, and desert, in certain works of fiction and poetry. See *The Enchafed Flood, or The Romantic Iconography of the Sea*, New York (1950). Water recurs in many of the quotations below.

the substance if not the idiom of the sense of anonymity and futility that is common to those who feel themselves to have been thrown into a world of chaotic power in which they have no meaningful part.

Another expression of this affection of generalized fearing or anxiety occurs in a letter written by John Donne between times of employment and before his ordination and "conversion" in 1608:

When I must shipwrack, I would do it in a Sea, where my impotencie might have some excuse; not in a sullen weedy lake, where I could not have so much as exercise for my swimming. Therefore, I would fain do something; but that I cannot tell what is no wonder. For to choose, is to do: but to be no part of anybody, is to be nothing. At most, the greatest persons, are but great wens, and excrescences; men of wit and delightful conversations, but as moalls for ornament, except they be so incorporated into the body of the world, that they contribute to the sustenation of the whole.[6]

Here, as in the case of Brainerd, we are impressed by the author's sense of powerlessness. Donne is a spectator of his own captivity to a lethargic will. He is powerless because he is purposeless, and he is purposeless because he is powerless to choose. Hence determination or resolution is not the cure for him.

A third example comes from Jean Paul Sartre's recollection of his childhood. He portrays it as a period of years during which he hid from himself, refusing to take responsibility for his own life, running away into his overfacile imagination.

A bewildered vermin, a waif and stray, without reason or purpose, I escaped into the family play-acting, twisting and turning, running, flying from imposture to imposture . . . . Good friends said to my mother that I was sad, that they had seen me dreaming. My mother hugged me to her, with a laugh: "You who are so gay, always singing! What could you possibly complain about? You have everything you want." She was right. A spoiled child isn't sad; he's bored, like a king. Like a dog. . . . This disgust is called happiness. My mother keeps telling me that I'm the happiest of little boys. How could I not believe

6. *The Life and Letters of John Donne,* vol. 1, 191.

it, *since it's true*. I never think about my forlornness. To begin with, there's no word for it.[7]

We are often tempted to discount men's memories of their distant childhood. In our recollecting there is usually some striving for effect. Nevertheless, whether Sartre is really presenting his early childhood or a later childhood born of his own adult reflections on human nature is somewhat beside the point. The passage is still descriptive of a human reality Sartre has known personally. Ostensibly what he speaks about here is not the same as the impotence of a mature man to follow a vocation, an impotence we have heard both Donne and Brainerd bewail. Yet, what Sartre evokes is a sense of powerlessness—the powerlessness that may assail us first of all in childhood but, as we know, also later on—to disentangle ourselves from the authority of other personalities. So this situation of a child is not basically different from the estrangement from purposiveness and self that the two earlier men expressed.

These three utterances come from the most diverse cultural and circumstantial origins. We cannot use them to postulate a necessary universal affection, but they do widen our understanding of the fearing, dreading frame of mind, when and where it occurs. Kierkegaard thought of dread as preeminently a "qualification of the dreaming spirit." In his book on dread and also in his other analyses and evocations of despair and doubting he focused attention on the individual in his solitary adventures into himself, on Adam discovering his freedom, on the Knight of Faith whose trust is wholly inward and concealed from all eyes. But Brainerd, Donne, and the philosopher-dramatist of existentialism enable us to see that what melancholy, forlorn, or dreading man suffers is not simply his own untried innocence or his trembling before the untold possibilities awaiting him. The man these writers know and describe suffers in a world—a world of alien purposes and agencies where he is weak, a world of solid bodies where he has no substance of his own, a world of persons

7. *The Words*, 93 f.

who direct themselves and one another while he lacks the capacity to direct himself. In each of these three cases, the writer is expressing his awareness that he has no innate, inalienable share in that which is most real to him, his own life-course.[8]

To recapitulate our understanding of fearing/dreading, we will distinguish the common elements that these examples have furnished us. First of all, we note as the salient mark of this affection the sense of powerlessness, which seems in fact to be not so much a felt absence of power as a sense of the presence of power that one is unable to annex to oneself or to master; "consciousness of Power without Strength" is the way in which

---

8. There are other examples too numerous to quote and analyze. Among those that are especially authentic and striking are the following: John Calvin's descriptions of the fearing state of mind in his chapters on providence in *The Institutes of the Christian Religion*, I. John Bunyan's many references to, and accounts of, his anxiety about salvation in *Grace Abounding to the Chief of Sinners;* Bunyan several times compares his powerlessness to that of a child; see par. 102 and par. 198. A paragraph of particular interest appears in Immanuel Kant's *Critique of Pure Reason*. It expresses the helplessness of ethical and religious man insofar as he is the captive of nature, the self-contained world of cause and effect. "We have now not merely explored the territory of pure understanding, and carefully surveyed every part of it, but also measured its extent, and assigned to everything in it its rightful place. This domain is our island, enclosed by nature itself within unalterable limits. It is the land of truth—enchanting name!—surrounded by a wide and stormy ocean, the native home of illusion, where many a fog bank and many a swiftly melting iceberg give the deceptive appearance of farther shores, deluding the adventurous seafarer ever anew with empty hopes, and engaging him in interprises which he can never abandon and yet is unable to carry to completion." Trans. N. K. Smith, London (1950), 257. Nothing could be further from a diary than the first *Critique*, but the language Kant uses here is dramatic and stands in the sharpest of contrasts with its context.

Also, S. T. Coleridge gives an account of his dreading as a child, which I have quoted above.

William James's *Varieties of Religious Experience* is, of course, the best single collection of verbal manifestations of dread, but the most interesting of all is James's account of his own experience, which he includes as the contribution of an anonymous Frenchman (toward the end of the chapter on the sick soul), because it is the most contemporary. Albert Camus' diary and notebooks include pertinent examples, such as his notes on the psychosis of arrest; see *Carnets 1942-1951* 4 f., to be read together with p. 37, on the accidental fragile nature of human relationships.

Dag Hammarskjöld's entries in *Markings* seem for the most part too self-consciously modeled on Kierkegaard when he touches on dread, but at least one such entry is noteworthy, the second dated Easter 1960.

Coleridge put it, "a perception, an experience, of more than ordinary power with an inward sense of Weakness."[9] Second, in the materials cited this affection reveals personal existence, to those whom dread and fear touch, as aimless, outside of any fixed coordinates, and the opposing world as an environment of randomness. Sartre theorizes that all emotions are the mind's efforts to construct an imaginary reality. On these grounds fear is the psychic energy that constructs a world in which flight is appropriate and that conceals the threatening world lying beyond one's power.[10] In the examples we have before us, dreading is the sense of lying foundered or idle in a word of chaotic power of stagnation. Third, fearing carries with itself a seed of the sense of guilt for this idleness and impotence—a sense well conveyed in Donne's characterization of himself as an "excrescence" and a "moall" on the body of mankind. And fourth, therefore, it makes the world appear to be inimical or disguisting: Sartre's description of his family as a company of play actors and Donne's calling the circumstances of his life "a sullen, weedy lake" embody this disgust.

Several commentators have chosen to call this frame of mind by the metaphorical name of shipwreck,[11] and as these examples

9. *Inquiring Spirit*, 40. Another passage Miss Coburn has taken from Coleridge's manuscripts illustrates what he described in these words: "I work hard, I do the duties of common Life from morn to night, but verily I raise my limbs, like lifeless *Tools!* The organs of motion and outward action perform their functions at the stimulus of a galvanic fluid applied by the Will, not by the Spirit of Life that makes Soul and Body one." *Ibid.*, 37.

10. *The Emotions, Outline of a Theory*, trans. B. Frechtman, New York (1948).

11. Herbert Read does so in *The True Voice of Feeling*, 184 ff. The context is a long note on Richard Woltereck's *Ontologie des Lebendigen*, in which Woltereck criticizes the exclusive preoccupation of Heidegger with *Angst* and Jaspers with *Angst* and *Scheitern*. Shipwreck is Read's translation of *Scheitern*. See Karl Jaspers, *Philosophie, Berlin* (2nd ed., 1948), 863 ff.

The frequency with which the image of shipwreck occurs both in the spontaneous entries of journals and in literary works in which the mood of anxiety is being evoked is connected with the natural efficacy of water as a symbol for defeating, destructive power. Beyond Donne's and Brainerd's use of it, the image of shipwreck occurs directly or allusively in Bunyan's autobiography (*Grace Abounding*, par. 186; also, of course, the "miry bog," par. 82), in Kierkegaard's *Journals* (the "*commune naufragium*," no. 163), suggest, it is an appropriate metaphor. Not only do the first two of the three men quoted use the image of men in distress on the water; all of them make the sense of isolation and alienation a chief characteristic of this resonance. The fragility and accidental nature of human relationships, the lack of substance or purpose, and hence of a real persona, stand out in these various descriptions.

Dreading where it appears and is named or described by the subject it afflicts is the condition of perceiving the world of power as being estranged from, and inimical to, the self. Not death alone but all things "disorder me." What is one, then, to make of this phenomenon that has been and is so widely recognized? Many questions press for answers in the light of this human reality. Is fearing/dreading a significant phenomenon or is it something epiphenomenal? This is a far-reaching question, but obviously a conviction underlying the whole of our presentation of faithful man in the radial world is that man *is* an affectional being and that his affectivity is significant. In particular, dread and fear indicate something as important about human beings as do the qualities of human religiousness and faithfulness. Is fearing a pathological condition, temporary and negative in its import for our understanding of "true" human nature? Or is it normal and normative, disclosing a universal feature of human existence? And if it is the latter, how then can it have any special meaning for Christians—as some commentators today maintain it has—or would-be Christians or post-Christians? Could

---

in William James's quotation from Jouffroy's personal account of his "counter-conversion" (*The Varieties of Religious Experience*, 173 f.), and in the following confession of Mussolini: "Yes, Signora, I am finished. My star is set. I still work, but I know that everything is farce. I await the end of the tragedy, strangely detached from it all. I don't feel well, and for a year have eaten nothing but slops. I don't drink. I don't smoke . . . . The agony is atrociously long. I am like the captain of a ship in a storm; the ship is broken up, and I find myself in the furious ocean on a raft which it is impossible to guide or to govern. No one hears my voice any more." John Toland, "Twilight of a Tyrant," *Look*, 18 May 1965.

The appearances of the image in literature are too many to list (see Auden's study for a beginning), but among the most forceful is Emily Dickinson's employment of it in her poem, "I felt a funeral in my brain": "And I and silence some strange race, / Wrecked, solitary, here."

we, for example, borrow the language of Calvin and Jonathan Edwards to say of this sense of being shipwrecked that it is a work of the Holy Spirit?

A developed theological reply to this latter series of questions would lead us into the complicated (and fascinating) topic with which Puritan pastors and theologians were especially concerned, the identifying marks of the indwelling Spirit of God. This is a topic we have not supplied and shall not develop. But if we respond only on the basis of the materials and theses we have so far presented, it is evident that certain approaches to the interpretation of fearing and dreading as religious affections are precluded.

First of all, it may well be true that we must distinguish between pathological and nonpathological fearing, although our conception of human health is forever changing. But our concern here is not with this particular distinction and the idea of being that those who use it defend or presuppose.[12] Instead, it is with the dreading that is common enough to be regularly recognizable as a condition and problem for men in each of the epochs of modern times, common enough so that we are ready to say with William James that those to whom it is unknown lack the "great initiation." What we know of human nature in these epochs, through ourselves and through the self-revelations of others, prompts us to affirm that dreading/fearing is far too conspicuous and pervasive a characteristic of existence in our world to be called epiphenomenal.

If, however, dreading and fearing are characteristic of human existence in our world, then there is a corollary, which becomes a second general observation. Sympathetic interpreters for Christianity speak amiss, when they reserve dread as a distinctively Christian phenomenon. Developing Kierkegaard's suggestions, some apologists have interpreted dread as a "negative" preparation for the reception of the gospel. They imagine it as a spiritual wasteland through which all men must pass on the way to faith

---

12. Paul Tillich made the distinction popular in theological anthropology. See *The Courage To Be,* New Haven (1952), chap. 3. It is correlated with his ideas of being and nonbeing.

through and in Christ. They dramatize fear as a condition that men are fully able to recognize and appreciate only after they have passed through it and beyond it, into a securer trust in God. But whatever qualifications we may add, the tendency to make anxiety a peculiarly Christian experience flies in the face of the facts that others have described for us. Theologians cannot ascribe dread to the Holy Spirit as a special preparatory work, unless as interpreters of affections they are willing to recognize the brooding of the Spirit in all men, without respect to their progress toward or away from the gospel.

Furthermore, whether as Christian interpreters or as some other kind, we cannot put dreading down as merely a "negative" or as a "preparatory" affection. Our examples and experience have shown that in dreading men apprehend something positive, the world of power that is in part antecedent to each one of us. Dreading shows, without doubt, a world or man-age that is opposing and that in its opposition is not only a defining but a limiting field of existence. Through dreading and fearing states the world appears in its identity as world that is not mine or ours. Rather, I and my generation belong to a field and an ambience over which we have no rights. Fearing is the perception of the immensity of power and of the weakness of any claims of ours. We could put fearing down as a merely negative affection, only if we restricted its significance to the meanings it discloses of the individual and his hopes or wishes. By its very nature, however, an affection is revelatory of the entire self-world polarity. While we are instinctively inclined, then, to see dread and fearing as a reflection of our own poverty, if we fully attend to what it opens to view, we perceive not merely emptiness but contrast: contrast between self and field of power, between small and great. Dreading is a revelation of infinite energy and of environing, shaping power that approaches us on alien terms. It is a revelation of what Coleridge called the "sacred horror" of existence.[13]

Finally, our observations and examples of man fearing and

13. *The Friend, The Works of S. T. Coleridge*, vol. 2, 464.

being anxious suggest a fourth general consideration respecting the revealing or disclosing powers of the affection. It is a consideration that has to do with the other data of experience we shall shortly be examining: fearing is not the single and sole affection that is revelatory of human existence in the world.[14] There are two psychological observations that are immediately relevant to this point. The first is the fact that an affection, a tonality, a *Stimmung* appears as something determinate, a state of despair or of melancholy or of equanimity, only to the extent that it contrasts with other specific states, either in memory or in present experience. To be capable of only one attunement in the world is to be incapable of any. One *Stimmung* having exclusive domain in human nature would be as uncommunicative and insignificant concerning human being, the human world, and the relation between, as would the power to make one judgment and one only about these things. Solitary facts that belong to no family of facts are silent.

But we find ourselves as subject to moods, not to a single encompassing mood, and this is the second psychological datum affecting our interpretation of the revelatory power of fearing. The fact that an attunement or affection draws its power of disclosure in part from the contrast it affords with other states of mind would be of only theoretical significance, were it not for the fact that man is more than anguish. His existence in the world breeds and augments another range of affections. Therefore, in describing the experience in which faith takes form in the field of power constituting our world we must move onward to describe and interpret another and opposing way of suffering: gladness.

14. The only criticism today of Heidegger's and Sartre's one-sided emphasis on anxiety or forlornness by a Christian philosopher comes from Stephan Strasser in his book, *Das Gemüt*. Strasser builds on the basis of previous phenomenology. Paul Tillich, of course, sets courage over against anxiety in *The Courage To Be* and faith in his *Systematic Theology*. But Tillich does not conduct any explicit criticism of Heidegger nor does he attempt to show the affectional nature of either anxiety or courage/faith. Among others who cannot be theologically identified, Otto Bollnow also criticizes Heidegger for neglecting the intensifying, exalting affections; see *Das Wesen der Stimmungen*.

III. Gladness

We have virtually no established language for our description of this opposing state of mind. There is, if anything, even less consensus here than there is for fearing. Nevertheless, we have in gladness as important a family of affections as fearing and its sister states of melancholy and despair. The apparently less evidential and striking character of gladness calls, however, for some comment, as we begin this second exploration.

First of all, the reader of such occasional literature as diaries and daybooks becomes aware that rejoicing expresses itself less directly than the opposing affection of shipwreck. Articulate manifestations are relatively infrequent. Why should this be so? One reason, perhaps, is that gladness and rejoicing issue more easily through channels other than the verbal. The most obvious of these alternate expressions is a man's work and the exercise of his ordinary abilities. Happiness, as Aristotle and other wise readers of human nature after him have observed, lies in the full use of one's powers. And if we think back on the examples of dreading that David Brainerd, John Donne, and Sartre provided, we recall that a significant occasion for the awareness of dread is the stifling of the power and freedom to produce and create. Consequently, one can theorize that the specific texture, as it were, and tangibility of rejoicing often come to attention only as a man looks back, during a period of weakness, to earlier days or hours when his mind was totally engrossed in some productive activity. But if rejoicing commonly occurs when a man is wholly engaged and not attentive to himself, so that memory is the principal mode of our conscious awareness of it, then another consideration suggests itself. The "gladness of joy" (to use Coleridge's most descriptive phrase) tends to merge with or become the background "tunning of the soul" that we take for granted while we are experiencing it. Both of these features are illustrated in a note that Coleridge has left behind for us:

Soother of Absence. Days and weeks and months pass on, and now a year; and the Sun, the Sea, the Breeze has its influence on me, and good and sensible men—and I feel a pleasure upon me, and I am to the outward view of all cheerful, and have myself no distinct consciousness of the contrary; for I use my faculties, not indeed as once, but yet freely. But oh Sara! I am never happy, never deeply gladdened. I know not, I have forgotten what the Joy is of which the Heart is full as of a deep and quiet fountain overflowing insensibly, or the gladness of Joy, when the fountain overflows ebullient.[15]

So gladness emerges in its distinctiveness most fully when it stands contrasted, through memory, with the presence of despair.

There is another feature of this phenomenon that we ought to note here, for it is illustrated indirectly in these same words by Coleridge. While there is no universally accepted nonmenclature for the glad affections, the words joy and gladness usually designate something different from simple pleasure or from intoxication and ecstasy. Joy, as this excerpt from Coleridge suggests and as Thomas Aquinas and Hobbes say explicitly, is an intellectual affection.[16] It belongs to the man whose mind is at work. On the other hand, it differs in a way that we shall see from beatitude or blessedness.

Our first example comes from Sartre's description of a later phase of his childhood:

I was beginning to find myself . . . . I was not yet working, but I had already stopped playing . . . . I was born of writing. Before that, there was only a play of mirrors. With my first novel I knew that a child had got into the hall of mirrors. By writing I was existing, I was escaping from the grown-ups, but I existed only in order to write, and if I said "I," that meant "I who write." In any case, I knew joy. The public child was making private appointments with himself.[17]

Sartre's irony throughout does not allow the reader to suppose

15. *Inquiring Spirit,* 61. Presumably this fragment dates from the period following Coleridge's well-known loss of his poetic creativity.

16. Aquinas recognizes joy as a specific kind of pleasure, pleasure as such being for him a general category in which both "brutes" and angels have a part. ". . . but the name of *joy* has place only as applied to that delight which follows upon reason." *Summa Theologica,* I, II[ae], Q XXXI, A III. Hobbes also makes joy the name of the "pleasures of the mind." His brief allusion to joy in chap. 6 should be supplemented with his discussion of dejection and melancholy among the "contrary defects" of the chief intellectual virtues in chap. 8 of *Leviathan.*

17. *Op. cit.,* 153.

that the work of writing cured him of forlornness. On the contrary, as he carefully reiterates, his writing was but a new method of elaborating lies about himself. Nevertheless, Sartre's language is of interest, for his brief mentions of joy, as opposed to his perennial forlornness, occur in connection with his activity of writing—an activity which he has never left off since his youth. It was through writing that he found liberation from his helpless entanglement in the personalities of his uncle and mother; writing focused his power and furnished him with some sense of substance. Sartre continues:

My vocation changed everything. I discovered that in belles-lettres the Giver can be transformed into his own Gift, that is, into a pure object. Chance had me a man, generosity would make me a book. I could cast my missive, my mind, in letters of bronze . . . . I could appear to the Holy Ghost as a precipitate of language . . . could, in short, be *other*, other than myself, other than the others, other than everything . . . . in order to be reborn, I had to write; in order to write, I needed a brain, eyes, arms.[18]

In a word, Sartre collected himself or found himself being collected and formed with a new solidity in the activity that brought him what he calls "my sacred joy."

The argument here is not that work makes a man happy but rather that the awareness of freedom to use one's powers is a perception especially associated with the frame of mind we call rejoicing. This aspect of the "gladness of joy" and certain other features appear more clearly in one or two entries in the daybook of Dag Hammarskjöld. "Not to encumber the earth" was the way in which Hammarskjöld expressed a deep desire, reminding us of Donne's opposing image of himself as an "excrescence" and "moall" on the body of mankind:

To exist in the fleet joy of becoming, to be a channel for life as it flashes by in its gaiety and courage, cool water glittering in the sunlight—in a world of sloth, anxiety and aggression.[19]

Again, in this entry, the suggestion of motion, energy, power

18. *Ibid.*, 193 f.
19. *Markings*, 67.

together with directionality of this energy as the felt content of the mood of rejoicing is unmistakable. There is another feature here also: the apparent dependence of the sense of "fleet joy" upon the contrast with the "world of sloth, anxiety and aggression." We will return to this. A third feature of the utterance, only implied in the words "to be a channel for life as it flashes by," is that rejoicing discloses the sense and conviction of being part of something larger, in this case, the river of life. Hammarskjöld is more explicit in another paragraph, written a year later, in 1952:

Now you know. When the worries over your work loosen their grip, then this experience of light, warmth and power. From without—a sustaining element, like air to the glider or water to the swimmer. An intellectual hesitation which demands proofs and logical demonstration prevents me from "believing"—in this, too. Prevents me from expressing and interpreting this reality in intellectual terms. Yet, through me flashes this vision of a magnetic field in the soul, created in a timeless present by unknown multitudes, living in holy obedience, whose words and actions are a timeless prayer.
—"The Communion of Saints"—and—within it—an eternal life.[20]

What is quite explicit in this effusion is the social metaphor, the presence of "unknown multitudes," which manages to suggest the double image of a solitude on which is superimposed companionship. It is noteworthy also that in this entry and in the preceding one the elements of water and air are friendly and sustaining of human power rather than turbulent and defeating.

There are more details of significance and other implications of the imagery that Hammarskjöld has used, but instead of attempting further comment on these words, we will take as a final example one of the most remarkable statements of rejoicing that we have in western literature surrounding the experience of faith—short of the writings of the mystics. It is Kierkegaard's entry in his *Journal,* dated May 19th., 1838, half-past ten in the morning. Although it is remarkable, it is also typical and recapitulates much of what we have already noticed.

20. *Ibid.,* 84.

There is an indescribable joy which enkindles us as inexplicably as the apostle's outburst comes gratuitously: "Rejoice I say unto you, and again I say unto you rejoice."—Not a joy over this or that but the soul's mighty song "with tongue and mouth, from the bottom of the heart": "I rejoice through my joy, in, at, with, over, by and with my joy"—a heavenly refrain, as it were, suddenly breaks off our other song; a joy which cools and refreshes us like a breath of wind, a wave of air, from the trade wind which blows from the plains of Mamre to the everlasting habitations.[21]

Language such as this on the part of a man who called melancholy his most intimate friend and mistress tempts one to dwell on each expression. We will note, however, only the paramount features of this outburst. First of all, here is manifest the foremost general characteristic of affections as such: the rejoicing comes over Kierkegaard, pervading both his world and his own sense of identity. It befalls him totally and without any particular commensurate cause.[22]

A second general though not universal feature of affection is exhibited in the note of abruptness with which the rejoicing overtakes Kierkegaard. He betrays himself as a man struck with the unfamiliar, with the absurdity (in the literal rather than pejorative sense of that word) of existence; but in this instance it is *gracious* absurdity: the pure, free givenness of personal existence in the world. So, we meet here a repetition of the amazement (astonishment, wonder) that the reader of the New Testament continually encounters in its accounts of the men and women who having ears hear or having eyes see the bursting life, the sudden power, the sharp judgment, and surprising liberty of which Jesus spoke in his parables. Astonishment pulsates in the Gospels, a psychic resonance of power in all the modes it touches men's hearts. It is not, to be sure, associated only with gladness and

21. *Loc. cit.*, no. 207.
22. Tchaikovsky writes, "Without any special reason for rejoicing I may be moved by the most cheerful creative mood, and *vice versa,* a work composed under the happiest surroundings may be touched with dark and gloomy colours." *The Life and Letters of P. I. Tchaikovsky,* ed. R. Newmark, London (1906), quoted by R. E. Harding in *An Anatomy of Inspiration and an Essay on the Creative Mood,* Cambridge (2nd ed., 1954), 368.

joy. The Gospel of Mark closes with a notation of the amazement and trembling of the women as they fled from the empty tomb; and Calvin reminds the reader of the *Institutes of the Christian Religion* of the "shaking and astoundedness" afflicting those who enter the presence of God without an appreciation of his immensity and their own littleness.[23] Astonishment is an exponent of quick translation from one existence-world into another. It is the accompaniment of discovery against the grain of anticipation. "The kings of the earth were gathered, and gone by together," says the Psalmist. "They marvelled to see such things; they were astonished and suddenly cast down."[24]

A third feature, peculiar to the affection of rejoicing, arrests attention in the way that Kierkegaard places himself on a landscape of time bounded retrospectively by the "plains of Mamre"

---

23. *Institutio Christianae Religionis, 1559*, I, 1, iii; *Joannis Calvini, Opera Selecta*, ed. Barth and Niesel, Munich (2nd ed., 1957), vol. 3. J. Glenn Gray writes about the astonishment that battle breeds in the following way: "When I could forget the havoc and terror that was being created by those shells and bombs among the half-awake inhabitants of the villages the scene was beyond all question magnificent. I found it easily possible, indeed a temptation hard to resist, to gaze upon the scene spellbound . . . . As I reflect further, it becomes clear, however, that the term 'beauty,' used in any ordinary sense, is not the major appeal in such spectacles. Instead, it is the fascination that manifestations of power and magnitude hold for the human spirit. Some scenes of battle, much like storms over the ocean or sunsets on the desert or the night sky seen through a telescope, are able to overawe the single individual and hold him in a spell. He is lost in their majesty. His ego temporarily deserts him, and he is absorbed into what he sees. An awareness of power that far surpasses his limited imagination transports him into a state of mind unknown in his everyday experiences . . . . This raptness is a joining and not a losing, a deprivation of self in exchange for a union with objects that were hitherto foreign." *The Warriors: Reflections on Men in Battle*, New York (Harper Torchbook, 1967), 33.

24. Psalm 48, vv. 3 f., Psalter of The Book of Common Prayer. Coleridge comments on the abruptness of transition between certain states of mind. ". . . Liking, Regard, Esteem, are continuous; and the Increase is so gradual as not to destroy the continuity. It is a^1 a^2 a^3 a^4. Love starts up or leaps in, and *takes place* of *Liking*. And even so it is, I suspect, with *Alienation*. There is a sudden *Death* of Love, or as sudden a Translation . . . ." Coleridge is speaking first of all about affections in which the will is deeply involved, but he connects this observation with the phenomenon of religious conversion. *Inquiring Spirit*, 60.—Paul Tillich, almost alone among recent theologians, made use of the phenomenon of astonishment, in a somewhat disguised fashion, in his well-known correlation of revelation and ecstasy.

and prospectively by "the everlasting habitations." As we have seen in other examples, joyfulness has to do with sharing, with meeting, with existence in society. The "plains of Mamre" are the place where Abraham pitched his tent and settled; where he built an altar to Jehovah; and where the angels of God appeared to him, and he gave them hospitality. "The everlasting habitations" is a phrase that explains itself. In Kierkegaard, then, joy takes on what biblical theologians would call an eschatological orientation. It expresses itself in the imagery of beginning and end—of the long history of Abrahamic faith. And this beginning and end require images of society. Whether deliberately or not Kierkegaard superimposes one image on another, existence in a family or city on solitude, and correspondingly one affection on another, gladness overlying melancholy. He depicts human life as motion between two societies. Thus joy gives temporal, historical depth to solitude, because it represents personal existence as existence from and toward others in the world.[25] It interprets human destiny as citizenship in an ultimate society, as membership in a cosmic body politic. This social imagery is not merely accidental. There seems to be a natural affinity between the sense of gladness and the immemorial image of the city. Friedrich Schleiermacher, who was also attentive to the tonalities of life in faith, was much aware of the close relation between joyfulness and the sociality of human nature. During a period of crisis and despair, the young Schleiermacher wrote to a friend:

With such friends as all of you are to me, it is not possible that I be defeated by any kind of grief; it must leave room for joy. Certainly, joy does not displace sorrow, but both overspread one's entire being, and I know right well that the joy emanates only from you, and from all that is fair . . . in myself alone I cannot keep it fresh and living. . .[26]

Taken in conjunction with Kierkegaard's words, this passage sug-

---

25. This age-old double perception of existence expresses itself in the collect familiar to users of The Book of Common Prayer: "Almighty God, our heavenly Father, who settest the solitary in families . . ."

26. *The Life of Schleiermacher, as unfolded in his Autobiography and Letters,* trans. F. Rowan, London (1860), vol. 2, 43 f. (Translation altered.)

gests why joy associates itself with the image of the city or family: joy is not individual; it tells of its origins beyond the single one. In Hammarskjöld's words, it arrives "from without—a sustaining element, like air to the glider, or water to the swimmer." "A magnetic field in the soul . . . created by unknown multitudes." In opposition to dread and fearing, rejoicing intensifies the awareness of sharing in the life and strength of others, and it underscores the sense of serving a cause in life and of having a contribution to make. The feeling, then, of belonging ultimately to the body of mankind or some family, of being destined for the everlasting habitations, is a feeling showing a distinctly moral character. It is a promise not only of the enjoyment of rights but of the power and freedom to be a contributor to the whole, to be a doer of deeds, an agent. It carries a promise of being recognized as a person.

If we pause now to look back over the ground we have covered, we see that rejoicing is properly defined as an affection opposing shipwreck. It entails consciousness of liberation into the stream of life, a sense of collectedness, a feeling of the union of one's own power with power and energy itself, and finally a sense of effectiveness and of recognition as an agent in a human commonwealth that transcends the present.

The most conspicuous feature, however, appears to be an inner sense of motion. Here also joy directly opposes dreading with the latter's attendant sense of stagnation. Spinoza defined the affection (*laetitia*) as "the transition of man from a lesser to a higher state of perfection."[27] Certainly, it seems to be inseparable from anticipation. But this is simply to say that rejoicing is a historical affection, like dread or fear. It requires resistance to come to birth in consciousness. Consequently, it is not the same as the state called beatitude or blessedness by medieval theologians, for it has the meaning to the person suffering it of "being under way," as Stephan Strasser has put it. The "gladness of joy" is attended

27. *Ethics*, pt. III, prop. LIX, "Definition of Affections of the Mind." (See S. Strasser's discussion of this transitional quality of joy in *Das Gemüt*, 233 ff.)

with tension.[28] In fact, we have to describe it as a form of mental distension, unlike the distractedness of dreading and fearing but still a state of mind involving restlessness and movement.

IV. Homo Duplex

Quite evidently rejoicing and dreading do not exclude each other. As Schleiermacher wrote: "Joy does not displace sorrow, rather both overspread one's entire being." This quality deserves stressing. Despair and dreading do not banish rejoicing, nor does gladness extinguish fearing. They are not contradictories; they are opposites and hence do not root each other out. So it is possible to be conscious at one and the same time of being "shipwrecked" and of "being under way." In his *Confessions* Augustine puzzled over this doubleness of the mind, "that when in a joyful mind I remember an earlier sadness, my mind hath joy, and my memory sadness" (X, xiv). It is a doubleness that pervades the whole book and shows how life can be appropriately portrayed as an oscillation between these two encompassing affections. Indeed, it seems to be almost a law of human existence (and this is partly the reason Augustine is so "modern" a man) that these two affections and their corresponding images are superimposed, and neither is likely to disappear completely. (We are, however, more aware of dread in joy than of joy in dreading.) And therefore all of a man's experiences are similarly deeply conditioned by these two tonalities of his being-in-the-world.

This doubleness of experience is so commonplace that we pass over it ordinarily as something trivial, perceiving in it at most merely a symptom of the internal temporal distension of our lives. We do not as a rule look to such everyday experiences as manifestations having an import for human destiny. And yet in disdaining

28. "At bottom life is beautiful only because of its tensions . . . . I recall only a few rare occasions that gave me a joy as tense as that which fills me now . . . . " Letter of Julius Leber from Lübeck prison; *Dying We Live,* ed. Gollwitzer *et al.,* trans, R. C. Kühn, London (1962), 155.

to place a theological or a religious interpretation upon the ordinary we commit an error. For it is just in this doubleness of experience that we meet and can trace, if we will, the geneses of some of the most influential beliefs of the church and—what is of more importance—can also win a greater understanding of the life in faithful experience that may appropriately call itself Christian.

For example, as we have just remarked, common experience in our world affords men both outside and inside the institutional church familiarity with the state of mind that is dreading and its sister, despairing. Less commonly or dramatically, perhaps, experience also gives men everywhere tastes of rejoicing and glimpses into that union of power and energy, direction and fate, which is gladness. But what neither these men and women nor professional theologians have recognized for a long while is that in this simple and terrible duality of existence lies the heart of the otherwise abstract, rather quaintly forensic, and nowadays lifeless doctrine of justification by grace through faith. The *simul iustus et peccator*, which Luther developed as a semitechnical comment on concrete personal experience but which later became a shibboleth of the doctrinaire in Christendom, is not an esoteric piece of Christian gnosis but an expression in legal-theological language of an experience accessible to every man who cares to attend to it, namely, that he is foundered and powerless and yet is on the way to membership in an ultimate society.

By itself, of course, the fact that the doctrine of justification by grace through faith still has an experiential root is not of great importance. Neither faith in general nor Christian faith in particular depends on this one doctrine. Such a reading of the experience of living in two worlds—the world of confusion and the world of order—with two personas—fear and gladness—suggests, however, that if we take the principal human affections more seriously, we may go much further into an understanding of faithful man in our present radial world and of the God that faithful men perceive than academic theology now permits us to go. What is of importance is the consequence that we may draw from the descriptions now before us: like all human faith Christian faith is a way of accepting the suffering that the world of power inflicts on men; it is a way of appropriating the experiences of diminution and enlargement, of distraction and motion, by interpreting them as twin moments in the ruling action of God. So the believing of God ruling human life generates in the suffering of power around and in oneself. Such believing does not, of course, spring unaided from such experience; it issues as the confessing of what men hold dear when they become convinced that their most authoritative predecessor in such experience was and is Jesus of Nazareth, who thought of his own life and then tried to teach others to see that life as the place where the ruling of God becomes apparent. But in turn this perception of Jesus' authority opens itself only to those who are willing to come in upon themselves and find that they are men affected in all that they think and do, needing to be widened in their understanding of what affects them.

chapter 5
The Age of God

Faith comes to birth in the binary of suffering and power. It is there that God appears. Therefore, we mislead ourselves if we define faithfulness as a property of our human nature. That would be saying too little about it, for such a definition would magnify the part of the sufferer in faithfulness but leave out of focus the field of suffering. On the other hand, to say that faith is a gift to men, something extrinsic and merely added to our natural capacities, is to slight the human pathos that generates faithfulness. Consequently, it seems more suitable to say that faithfulness is neither a property of, nor an endowment superadded to, our constitution, but rather it is a trait of enworlded man. It is a trait of the binary.

I. The Axes of Faithfulness

When faith appears and forms, it shows itself as conduct in an age. It shows itself as fear or as hope or as both fearing and hoping together. It shows itself in the mental energy of thinking and believing. It appears as speaking, as listening, and as other kinds of action that probe the paths of power. Correspondingly, a man's understanding of his own faith-conduct draws heavily upon his perception of the pattern and the scope of the field of power in which he finds himself engaged. And the name that he gives to his faithfulness is often a name he takes from the particular being or beings in his world that most compellingly embody and show true beauty or goodness or justice. He takes for a surname of his own identity in faith the name of the being who authorizes and warrants his share in true power.

When, for example, in the past times and places of our predecessors that we call the age of belief or the era of the schoolmen, faith principally signified the assenting response of the mind to statements about God and the origins of being and salvation, it did so because men had in view as their opposing and encompassing world the nurturing, teaching action of the church, the city of God on earth. Faith became definite as the individual claimed his share and took his place in the field of action by joining his assent to the holy fathers' teaching of tradition and the mother church's great consensus. Men assumed the name of Holy Catholic Christians. Such assenting and asserting of membership in an eternal society of truth is still the distinguishing mark of faith to many.

In a parallel way, when and where faith has meant a right reading of the Bible and an attentive listening to the preacher's exposition and application of the text, it has done so because men perceived the surrounding action-world as an epic history of covenants: of prophecies, commandments, and assurances. The Book of Covenants was their mainstay through all turmoil and their charter for the future. And faith was not only attentive hearing and enactment of divine directives and mandates. It was—and is—courageousness, resolution, and liberty to reform, to begin again, to venture, and to create. Men assumed, in keeping with their experience, the names of the symbols of these promises, mandates, and assurances, calling themselves Reformed Christians, Baptists, Covenanters, and so forth.

Similarly, human faith has repeatedly taken the form of communion with the sources of life. It has done so whenever men have become aware of the forces around them and in them as elements of a strong and inexhaustible unity embracing all things. Faith-conduct in such a world is, for example, recognition that the common issues of life present parables about the whole. It is feeding on the Bread of Life in the satisfaction of physical hunger. It is return to the eternal originating One through meditation on a mundane name or place. Faith of this kind goes by appellations that signify the communicants' conviction about the sacramental nature of all being: eucharistic faith, mystical faith, ascetical faith.

The names that faith has borne, even within Christendom alone, have been many; and while the reasons for that fact are themselves numerous the most significant has been the differences in kind of the actions that men have perceived as the action shaping their world and themselves: the action of Truth establishing and sustaining intellectual order; the action of Providence encouraging men along their ways; the action of Eternity infusing mortal beings with immortality.

Perhaps the most striking, the most dramatic, and certainly a profoundly symbolical element in these differing axes of perception of power is the variation among the ideas of Jesus as the Christ that have successively regulated men's field of vision in Christendom. Each epoch and type of Christian faithfulness has centered its mind on one dominant image of Jesus. And that image, in turn has always presented two aspects: one aspect being exemplary of the circumpressing action of the field of power and the other exemplary of the patience or suffering that best sustains, appropriates, and responds to the circumpressing action. In the world perceived as a Logos-formed world, for example—that is, as a world that is the precipitate of God's thinking or Reason—Christ stands out as the Logos enmanned and at the same time as a teacher living in purity of heart under the very Truth he embodies. In the world that is the history of God covenanting, Christ is the Testament of God's steadfastness in action, and he is also the exemplar of man relying totally on

God's promises. In the visible order of man and nature that represents to the human eye the invisible and ineffable One, Christ is the perceptible glory of God, the majesty, beauty, holiness, kindness, and justice of God in determinate form; and he is also the man who prays—as all others ought but do not—for a share in the glory he demonstrates.

And so not only have the names of faith been many, and many also the kinds of shaping action perceived in faith, but the images of Christ as the theater of that action and as the forerunner of faithful conduct in the theater of action have similarly been many. Moreover, since human faith itself is rarely simple, and since human vision is never single, these differing correlations of faith, power, and Christ do not succeed each other in pure serial form, but instead they overlap and overlie and reflect and refract one another and live on in one another.

Each of these binaries of suffering and power, these faith-worlds with their exemplary Christs, has risen, waned, and on occasion waxed again—some of them many times. All of them are still discernible, if not in full power, in vestigial form. But none is now in ascendancy. None of them is wide and strong enough to hold the experience that shapes, augments, accelerates, and deflects radial man in his radial world. Each of them does suggest to sympathetic observation or to the trained historical imagination how men did and might identify themselves as followers, as imitators, or as participants of Jesus in a shared time and field, but none has the vitality to assert itself again as encompassing reality in the present. Their inability to do so betrays itself in the great and expanding distance that men of the present sense between themselves and their predecessors. The kinds of experience in this radial world that foster this sense of distance are familiar.[1] There are few men today who are not conscious of their alienation from the past. It is an estrangement, moreover, that no scholarship or historical craft can wholly heal. The correlation between the teaching church and minds assenting is too commonplace in a world that burdens men with too much knowledge and too many memberships in too many societies dedicated to

1. See chap. 1.

information and education. The correlation between the Bible and faith courageously obeying its mandates and commandments is too brittle in a world whose nations act out histories that did not originate in the story of Abraham's covenant. The correlation between sacramental life and men seeking communion seems too parochial in an age that strains outward to the stars for signals of strange life while life on earth burgeons and outpaces its own support. These former worlds have passed from strength to dependence.

Since neither church nor book nor sacrament can symbolize or convey the patterns of power in the present, how are we to interpret the inchoate faithfulness trying to take form in this age? May radial man accept for himself the name of Christian? Does Jesus of Nazareth warrant and strengthen faith-conduct among today's generations? Is there, beyond the worlds that have passed, another world in process, a world that Jesus may be said to have entered as a pioneer?[2] a world that radial men with their distinctive rhythm of perception may see as a new theater of action in Jesus as well as in themselves? Is there a living world, not yet consigned to memory or tradition, that they may share with him as a new beginner of faithfulness?

It is plain that if there is such a world available it can be only the present radial age. And if the present does hold such a possibility it is also certain that it must show itself as a larger world than any men have hitherto assimilated. It must offer a wider correlation between faithful existence and the field of action shaping faith. It must offer more than vestiges of earlier piety and more than promises of future piety still immature. It must disclose patterns of augmenting and directing power in which men are *now* caught up, in which men are *now* suffering, are *now* fearful, are *now* glad. It must glint with newnesses, promptings of metanoia, and signs of glory, which men *now* worship, whether secretly or openly.

If the present does hold such possibilities, then we need to

---

2. Pioneer is a familiar rendering of the title that The Letter to the Hebrews (12:2) gives to Jesus. Archegos: beginning, founder, prince, first cause, etc.

explore it not only as a product of past Christendoms or as an earnest of future religion but as a new world arising and exhibiting traits of faithfulness that even past epochs had long forgotten and failed to realize and that the future is still powerless to beget. And the exploration of the present in this vein must strive for two goals, for the discovery of two features of experience by which we may orient ourselves. The first is the discovery of something that is common to Jesus of Nazareth and to radial humanity. This search is not for an effect in our contemporary social, cultural, or intellectual milieu of which we may say that Jesus is its remote or ultimate cause. It is rather a search for something given both in Jesus' situation and in our own. It is a search for something common to him and to us as men, for something shared. It is a search for a true common third.

The second goal is the discernment of a fellowship that cannot be counted merely as something given or something shared by virtue of a common situation. The second goal is rather the goal of apprehending the fellowship between Jesus of Nazareth and radial man—the spontaneous kinship of like-mindedness—that forms in and through the recognition of this common third. It is the goal of understanding what it was in Jesus's engagement with his times that made him a forerunner and a new beginning of faithfulness in his world and also of understanding what it is in present experience that prepares men to translate Jesus to the captaincy of their own suffering.

These two objectives are objectives of one search. Neither will stand out in sufficient relief unless the other also appears in clarity great enough to give depth and a horizon for the eyes' perspective.

II. The Common Third

The common third is God. It is—to paraphrase the language Jesus used—God-Ruling. The common third appears in the following way.

Beyond the correlation of the church and man assenting; beyond the correlation of the book and man attending; beyond the correlation of the sacrament and man communing, there stands another. It is the correlation between power in its infinite forms and human being as totally affected being. This correlation embraces a much broader commerce than the former three. It is the correlation between light, sound, and energy in its many modes and human being as perceiving being. It is the correlation between beauty and pleasure. It is the correlation between great regulative ideas and images and the mind's action. It is the correlation between coercive and persuasive power assailing radial man and the particular ways in which he shares in, and surrenders himself to, that assailing power.

But in order to perceive this wider field and our commerce with it, we must awaken to it, not only in our senses or in our willing or in our reasoning but also in our affections of fear and gladness and in the other resonances of power that range between them. When we have awakened in this way, we are better able to understand the effective authority that church, book, and sacrament possessed in former times and still exercise in lesser strength. We are able to understand how they exercised great authority, augmenting and directing men's lives, because they represented and focused this wider field. They borrowed and thereby symbolized an authority not their own. And since they did so and do so, they were and are also able to distract attention from that which they symbolize and so to mute and obscure the power that invigorates them.

Examples of this dependence of church, book, and sacrament on the wider field of power are not far away. One that is familiar to the reader of the New Testament—be he casual or intent reader—comes in the letters of Paul, the apostle of Christ to the Greek and Roman worlds. It comes not in the text alone but in the letters as messages and vehicles of Paul's meaning across space and time. These letters are filled with counsel and directions concerning the conduct of those in Corinth, Galatia, Philippi, and elsewhere who follow Christ, trying to translate his conduct of self into the field of their own lives. These letters bristle with instructions about marriage and sexual behavior, about attitudes toward Jewish and pagan laws, about responsibility to the Roman state, and about many other matters. Even more conspicuously in the letters, there swarm great and vivid images of life in time and space as seen under the aspect of Jesus of Nazareth crucified and risen. Here the reader and the auditor meet the two Representative Men, the First and the Second Adam. Here also the reader and the auditor come before the sacramental Body of Christ, the church; the Being-in-the-Form-of-God who emptied himself to become formed as a man; the Tribunal of God that declares the Guilty to be Righteous. These letters with their creedal, hymnic, mythic tributes to the name of Jesus are the implements with which Paul broadcast the seeds of Christ-formed conduct and thinking across men's imaginations.

However, these dramatic instructions, threats, and encouragements could not have won regard, even from their first readers, had they not swelled with a prior and larger reality; just as today the letters do not really engage us unless they remind us of, and appeal to, something beyond both apostle and church. It was a reality that Paul himself knew well, so well, evidently, that he seems often to have forgotten it in his attentiveness to the moment. Yet he wrote always from within its grasp: the grasp of the power that shapes men, driving them where it will, as it drove Jesus into the desert to pray, into Galilee preaching, and into Jerusalem to die; the grasp of the power that outside Damascus contradicted Paul's first way of thinking and acting and made him its speaker in the cities of the Diaspora and its translator among the gentiles.

The power that enlivened Paul's images and augmented his preaching and teaching was the power that endowed Paul and his readers with a commonalty. Moreover, this commonalty that Paul shared with his readers and parishoners was a commonalty he held with them as men who were already sharing this possession—or, better, this being possessed—with Jesus, "the first born" of men, the "pioneer of faith." This commonalty is the locus of Paul's authority. Here is the origin of Paul's claim and command among men. It is in the power that directs, augments, and diminishes all life. The letter, the homily, or the personality in which such power appears "has" authority, because it is itself shaped and directed by the authorizing power that encompasses the entire field of action. The weight Paul's letters carried and carry actively bears upon men when and where they take and read them with the double insight, born of experience: (1) that that which afflicts and affects the writer affects the reader also; and (2) that being about whom the writer speaks is a being also and above all so afflicted and shaped. Hence, the structure of experience that endows Paul's communications with so much more than a merely individual charisma or even institutional credit is triangular. The authority appears in the shared experience of the first, the second, and the third persons of the communication. It appears to the reader *inwardly* as he recognizes the suffering out of which Paul writes (the sense of being constrained and directed) to be analogous to his, the reader's, own sensibility and as he recognizes the suffering out of which Jesus acts to be a transfiguration of such suffering. But this authority discloses itself *outwardly* also in the analogous ways that persuasive and coercive power publicly befall the persons of the communication. The pattern lived out by Jesus, the pioneer and perfecter of faith, becomes authoritative for the reader, in Paul's letters, as it interprets the commonalty binding writer and reader together: the undergoing of diminution and enlargement.[3]

The watchfulness and believing that seize such images and precepts as informed Paul's discourse arise in this early, universal level of experience. The ideas of God and man that Paul shared with his fellows are the sublimations of these kindred affections. The communion in the Body of Christ, Paul's church, is rooted in the more ultimate fellowship of kindred pathos in the one embracing field of power. The assurance of surmounting with Jesus all the enmities opposing men in life and death, Paul's good news,

3. Philippians 2:1-11, the passage containing the great kenosis hymn, displays this structure particularly clearly: ". . . complete my joy by being of the same mind, having the same love, being in full accord and of one mind . . . . Have this mind among yourselves, which you have in Christ Jesus, who, though he was in the form of God . . ." (RSV).

is an assurance that issues from men's perception of the same action in their world/age as that which bore Jesus to his goal. The cosmos-encompassing Savior, whom Paul represented with his pen, and the exemplary Christ-Spirit of purity, for whom Paul acted as plenipotentiary in church discipline, draw their reality and their efficacy from the positing, defining, ruling action that became visible in Jesus of Nazareth and those who ate with him and recognizable, thereafter, as the action that shapes all men.

Here is the common third for Paul and his readers in Corinth and in Rome, in Burundi, Memphis, and Kent. This ruling action, present to the numbed and distracted mind in pathos and to the awakened mind in affective faith, makes Paul and his discourse intelligible to others.

The circumstances in which the Johannine writings, the history of the Acts of the Apostles, and all of the other literary works of the early church succeed in presenting reality to men under the aspect of Jesus Christ are not different. They are all dependent on this common third by which the I (of the author) and the you (of the reader), the we (of the author and reader together) and the he (of the letter or narrative), are bound together. These works are all mimeses of the polarity of pathos and power as it is focused in Jesus's conduct of himself in the theater of God-Ruling. Everything that evangelist and apostle attempt to do and to say in the new communities of Christ-minded men lives in this correlation. Outside it their images fade. There are no eyes to see. Their doctrines have no resonance. There are no ears to hear. The mystical social Body of Christ is not real to men unless they are men who can identify their own struggling to manage the life of their own bodies with their prizing of the history of the individual body, Jesus of Nazareth. In turn, the history of Jesus, his achievements and defeats, are not real to men, unless they can set their own experience of the resistance of the field through which they walk alongside their admiration of Jesus' motions as full of grace and truth. But the time and space of Jesus' conduct are not real to men unless they are men who can perceive themselves as beings compressed and formed by the same prevenient power as affected him.

So we come again to the recognition of the meaning of the common third. Outside the experienced polarity of suffering and power, expanded and intensified into the correlation of striving faith and encompassing rule, the precepts, images, and ways of Christ-influenced life give the impression of being rote responses in an outworn catechism and mechanical gestures in a rite rehearsed too often.

Words have no mass and momentum of their own, any more than does a body outside its field of gravity. These properties belong to them only when they in turn belong to a general field of experience and meaning. In every age there are always some words that drift on the surface of a people's speech without truly belonging to the patterns and currents of meaning that energize the language as a whole. Such is often the case with old words and stories. Today, the writings of the early Christian authors drift much of the time on the surface of our language, outside the patterns of our experience. It is only when these writings, through some insight born of accidental juxtaposition or intensive examination, touch the nerve of a reader's deepest affection that they become living symbols again of the universal bond of pathos and power.

To understand what such authors as Luke and Paul meant, the reader must be touched and awakened to himself as a man entered by the same action as that which ruled in Jesus, endowed Saul of Tarsus with the persona of Paul the apostle, and transformed Luke the onlooker into a historian sharing in the history he recorded. Paul's or Luke's meaning finds a corresponding perception only in an awareness like that from which it issued: the awareness that spread and spreads among men who acknowledge themselves in the aftermath of Jesus as beings similarly affected and as members of the same race. Apart from such awareness of common suffering, there can be no helpful comparison of self with other. The author Paul would have no access to his readers. The reader in Philippi would have no access to Paul the author. And neither author nor reader would have access to Christ. In turn, without such comparison the members of the communication would share in no reflective, imaginative, dispositional, and animating identificaton with one another. And apart from such identification, the self idles in its own exigency, needful of a persona yet drowsy and unformed. Consequently, when faith seeks faith by words or any other symbols, the undertaking demands the presence in the communication of the common third. Outside the binary of suffering and power there is only incomplete comprehension.

The communication depends upon the felt presence of this binary. The endeavor, therefore, to read or to listen to these old words about Jesus in his age and to translate him from thence into our world or ourselves from here and now into his age involves far more than any care or even piety can supply. No word or deed can summon the unbound power that elicits from men their answering suffering, any more than could the words of Israel's prophets summon Yahweh. It was rather Yahweh's presence burning in the prophets' bones that expelled out of them the living word or sign.

Yet there is one "place" in the culture of Christianly employed language which, though not a summons, is a more nearly direct and a more spirited and forceful expression of the common third than any other. This "place" is the idiom of the Synoptic Gospels, most particularly the account Mark gives of Jesus and his companions, but also the Gospels of Luke and Matthew. The polarity of power and suffering is the very heart of the matter appearing in the voices of these narratives, as they speak of *basileia* (rule) and *metanoia* (changed, transformed mind), of *dunamis* (power) and *phobos* (fear), of *exousia* (authority) and *thaumasmos* (astonishment), of *doxa* (glory.) and *chara* (joy). Recognition of this polarity in these voices is, of course, not automatic. It is subject to the same conditions that govern meaning generally in the vocabulary of religion and faith. These terms also perform their work only when they are wedded to perception and name features of a field that presses in upon the senses of the body and the mind. The mere familiarity of *kingdom* or *rule*, of *power* and *authority*, of *repentance, fear,* and *gladness,* is not an aid, especially when these words that Christendom has repeated daily for

so many centuries name features of experience that have eroded
or subsided into latency in the world in which men reiterate them.
But this synoptic language *may* become an occasion of insight and
recognition when a tremor in the body of mankind, a slippage in
the crust of manners and habits, or a change in the watersheds
of thinking begins to uncover a different human world, one in
which the buried and forgotten stand out again and new land-
marks appear, providing visible features for the overly familiar
signs and sounds to name again in an unfamiliar manner.
Jesus' speaking about the ruling of God in power, in authority,
in astonishment, and in fear may manifest the common third, as
it has done before, when it collides with the shifting perceptions
of men in a fluxing present and fuses with them to create the
space of a new human world. Hence, Mark and the other accounts of Jesus as the messenger of an unrecognized universal
rule and as the author of new-mindedness carry a potential credibility in the ear of radial man that is distinctive. The credibility
accrues from the fact that these accounts, more than any other
voices of past witnesses and interpreters of Jesus, can be sensibly
consonant with the tenor and dissonance of a world in which
power is salient, with the circumstances of the age of radial man.

Our reasoning here involves three steps. (1) The synoptic language conveys the perception of the world/age that Jesus shared
with his friends. (2) It also designates, as the foregoing para-
graphs have suggested, the commonalty on which Paul's efforts
were dependent, as well as all similarly intended effort in that
first Christianly perceived world. (3) And, beyond that, it can
also afford insight into the common third between Jesus of Nazareth and our radial humanity, insofar as that language fuses
with our own perceptions. The language of these Gospels, reach-
ing into our world as a communication, offers a connection that
we do not otherwise easily see and name: the *basileia tou theou*,
God-Ruling = the action defining Jesus and issuing in his conduct and speech = the commonalty of all men who suffer
diminution and enlargement in the polarity of power and
pathos = the common third of past and present experience.

Our argument here is not that this equation is self-evident. Self-evidentness is a quality of a field of perception and of a way of seeing. And our perception is overtaxed, inhibited, and too much stylized. It is inhibited by the complexity of modern historical consciousness. No piety that is honest with itself can, for example, conceal the fact that the phrase Kingdom of God is something of an archaism in our world. This translation of *basileia tou theou*—a rubric that our grandfathers' Bibles showed in red ink—can and does bring about misunderstanding simply because it prompts an anachronistic or too literal hearing of Jesus' speech as the Synoptic Gospels give it to us, and so it can obscure rather than clarify the common third of which we are in search. Perhaps such a danger is obvious to men grown deft in the techniques of historical interpretation, but even historical science cannot regulate the meanings of words; it can only warn against misuse.

To be sure, Kingdom of God cannot *cause* misreading of the Gospels, but it can be the *occasion*, when men react by focusing their attention on the despotic, imperial, and monarchical forms of government in the history of East and West and by rejecting the image as time bound and not fitting to a race of autonomous beings. The theologian of the social gospel, Walter Rauschenbusch, took just such offense, because Kingdom of God appeared to him to liken men to subjects rather than to citizens. Of course, such a reading lacks the ironic sense, failing as it does to see that whatever the great differences may be between government by one and government by all, the swift and unpredictable history of nations still befalls men abruptly and painfully, however ample their franchise. Moreover, such reading also lacks a sense for the metaphorical nature of Kingdom of God in the Gospels. Nevertheless, no amount of care can entirely expunge the archaism of the image.

Conversely, if men seize too eagerly its metaphorical nature and spiritualize the image too much, they easily hide from themselves the actual temporal, cultural, and psychological distance separating the evangelists' history from their own. Therefore, no man inclined to read the parables and sayings of the Kingdom with sympathy can afford to ignore what scholars have admonished the reader today to bear in mind. The culture that helps shape the evangelists' accounts is a distinctive and unrepeatable culture. The tempo of their hopes and fears does not agree with modern time. Their language is theirs alone. The civilization— the protoscience, the art and craft, the social organization—supporting them is not the civilization of radial man. The mores of the Marcan or Lucan or Matthaean societies are not the mores of the present day. In these ways and in many others, the Gospels concerning Jesus as the herald of God-Ruling are remote, and no academic reconstruction of those times can make them our times. Instead, a great and irreducible distance divides that world from this one, just as a great human as well as geographical distance divided the Corinth and Rome in which Paul moved from the Galilean scene known to the first tellers and recorders of the acts and sufferings of Jesus.

But historical distance and unlikeness do not exhaust for us the import of this language. Whatever misapprehensions overtake us in reading Kingdom of God, there is an efficacy in the matter the image symbolizes that makes this image or its equivalent indispensable to religion and faith. It is the efficacy of the concrete experience of all mankind, the experience of freedom within an embracing unfreedom, the endeavor to discover or devise a government of self and of man with man within a general government of things that human government did not create. Kingdom of God is a deathless image because it expresses the experience that has always caused the family, the tribe, the city, and the nation to look for the pattern of power that makes their destiny and that has always required of them that they search out in their lives the felt continuum of earth, heart, and altar. It is an ultimate metaphor, and the experience that it draws into itself and fuses is illimitable. The phenomena of power and fear, of authority and amazement, of glory, sublimity, majesty and gladness are not features of simply one language and culture. For as any radial man who is able to read his own life can testify, what these terms signify has as much place in his own experience as in the world of the Gospel writers.

The energy invigorating the synoptic narratives, the fear—of evil and of good—the astonishment, and the opened mind that breaks into speech—all of these things also appear and resound in the world of today's reader. Like the congregation in the synagogue of Capernaum, like the centurion asking that his servant be healed, like the Samaritan woman drawing water for a thirsty Jew, and like the timid, overconfident Simon Peter, the reader too is an affective and affected being.

Therefore, opposing the risks that accompany an ignorance or forgetfulness of the wide differences between that world and this, there is a contrary misunderstanding that may interject itself. It is blindness, born of the fear of modernizing, to the analogies that lie side by side with the differences between that experience-world and our own. This contrary misunderstanding is an insensibility to the qualities common to life then and now: the dreadful knowledge that men cry "Peace!" but there is no peace; the recognition of the implacable evil on earth, which no society can subdue; the hope that is disillusioned, poisoned by resentment and yet stubborn for a larger and more generous life together; the deep knowledge that men and nations must repent intertwined with the sullen refusal of the cost of repentance; the horror and amazement at remote, small consequences of deeds that have secretly crept near and grown large; the blindness to the silent springs of life; the apathetic acceptance of the earth's daily hospitality; the tyranny of the fear of decay, and the "terror of history."[4] Affected in all of these ways, the race of radial man seeks signs of an original and underived, of a generous and indestructible government rooted in the Power that empowers life, which will make self-government for men and nations possible.

Therefore, along with whatever historically visible continuities and discontinuities there may be between radial man and the first auditors of Jesus' good news, there are common affections. They are affections clearly or obscurely responsive to a common affect-

4. The phrase is Mircea Eliade's. See *Cosmos and History*.

ing power that appears in human powerlessness and in the accompanying "consciousness of Power without Strength." It is in them that the common third shows itself most sensibly to men. It is this commonalty that enables the member of radial humanity to come together with the narrative he reads. Borrowing from the science of interpretation, we may say that it is this commonalty that provides the indispensable help to right understanding, the key for opening the meaning of what other men are saying. Under the rule of the common third, this coming together of the reader and the reading initiates in the resonance of common affections arising from similar experiences and revealing common realities and meanings in fields of action that otherwise are isolated by historical distance and social space. Under the same rule, the action of coming together issues in a colliding and a coalescing of the world of the reader with the world of the narrative, the world of the auditor with the world of the tellers, the world of the onlooker with the world of the actor, so that the accounts of Jesus and his followers become intelligible because they become credible as moments of a presently experienced world. For, again, as that man knows who reads his own life while he reads the evangelists, what the accounts of Jesus and his disciples and companions present is a series of episodes of human sufferings and awakenings to the character of the environing age, the age of judgment and new life, especially as that age appears in Jesus himself. The Gospels present the histories of men's conversions—and failed conversions—from their former ways to a share in the world of Jesus' perception and conduct. They are histories of men being called to arise from sleep to see in their own diminutions and unlooked-for enlargements the finger of God pressing them, directing them, correcting them, and enforcing their lives in the pattern typified and made concrete in Christ.

The beginnings of determinate faith appear in these Gospels, then, as they appear in the radial world: not primarily in concepts of God or in dramatic acts of obedience or in other special or ritual moments—although these have their place—but most noticeably in men experiencing, viz., going through the space and time allotted to them, and coming to perceive their world as the place of God-Ruling, where they themselves are being unmade and made anew as a part of that ruling action. Faith emerges not fully formed but in intermittent discernments and halting actions encouraged by the example of prophet, saint, and pioneer in whom the power shaping human life appears as a persona in the theater of its own rule. The new-mindedness to which Jesus called men, the metanoia about which the evangelists so often speak, is such a process and—occasionally—a progress in which the undergoing of sorrow and gladness in the power-world is resolved and refounded as the experience of the ruling God.

While, therefore, there are many kinds of distance now making the first followers of Jesus' way an almost infinitely remote people, there is a bond to tie the present-day reader to the actions and events recounted in the evangelists' history. It is the bond of suffering that may clarify into a perceiving, the bond of seeing that both in first-century Galilee and in the country around Jerusalem and in the age of radial humanity men feel and conduct themselves as estranged from power and outside of all pattern or government or they acknowledge the presence and authority of such power not according to the kind of space that is measurable in physical or temporal or cultural terms alone but according to the space of their own affections.[5]

III. The Age of God

The Gospels represent Jesus of Nazareth as a God-shaped man. On this all agree, synoptic and Johannine witnesses alike, and Paul's letters give us the same sense.

Of course, within this agreement stand wide disagreements

5. See Augustine's *Confessions*, trans. W. Watts, *The Loeb Classical Library*, Cambridge (1950) I, xviii. "For I had straggled far away from thy countenance in the mistiness [darkness: tenebroso] of my affections. For we neither go nor return from, or to thee, upon our feet, or by distances of spaces: nor did that younger brother seek post-horses, or waggons, or ships, or fly away with visible wings, or take his journey by the motion of his hams, that living in a far country he might prodigally waste that portion . . . . he went from thee out of a voluptuous affection; that is to say, a darkened one; and such is that which is far from thy countenance."

between the symbolisms these sources indicate as foremost in Jesus' action and being. In modern times scholars have recognized and made much of this fact. Theological interpreters of these findings have tried in turn to give an account of the disagreements between the different Christs and have offered two principal explanations. The first is to the effect that Jesus of Nazareth is Christ to men as they behold him with eyes of faith. Since men awaken into faithfulness in different ways, from different dreams and depths of slumber, they see Jesus in correspondingly different lights. The second explanation affirms that the features common to all of the representations of Jesus are more important than the disagreements. These two theological accounts are clearly not incompatible, and men combine them in virtually endless ways and present them in equally infinite degrees of persuasiveness. Conversely, others greet this diversity with skepticism, again in varying degrees, and parry the theological apologies with corresponding wit. This dialectic between the constructors of Jesus' life and personality and the critical voices of doubt, having once begun, has never abated and promises never to stop.

But to the man struggling for a whole persona, in which actions, words, and attitudes will show some coherence and agreement with the "grain" of things, the variety in the "portraits" of Jesus,[6] the apologies for that variety, and the critical dissolutions of these apologies are not immediately important matters, though in time he must acknowledge them.[7] What is most immediate and ultimate to such a man is the matter of God: the matter of a universal rule to which he belongs and the matter of a locus, a life, a persona in which the action of universal ruling appears. The questions he carries to his meetings with the biblical appearances

6. Portrait is an unhappy name for the kind of representations of Jesus the Gospels furnish. Montage would be more apposite to the effect the evangelists achieved.
7. The relation of these immediate questions to the scholarly problems that the history of the texts poses receives a great deal of attention among theologians. Paul Tillich and Rudolf Bultmann are, perhaps, the two best known. Two helpful books are John Knox's *Criticism and Faith*, New York (1952) and Van A. Harvey's *The Historian and the Believer*, New York (1966).

of Jesus are large indeed and no more manageable than are the other great practical questions of his life. "Is there a ruling of life here that is God?—Let the variety and the disagreements be. Let the explanations and critical doubts concerning the portraits clash. The care these Christ-images touch in me is the care for a recognizable God. Does this beginner and beginning of 'Christian' faithfulness belong to a pattern of power that I may recognize as a ruling in my own life also?" The final issue of this practical concern will depend on the outcome of the collision or—more likely—on the outcome of the many collisions that occur when radial man reads his own life while he is reading the accounts of Jesus as the Christ among some citizens of Jerusalem, of Antioch, and of other regions of that world.

Consequently, this double reading is a phenomenon that, though it also is commonplace and occurs unnoticed daily, deserves some recognition and interpretation as an important and complex event, in which much moral energy is aroused, redirected, and released.

Such a double or reflexive reading is a transaction in several senses. First of all it is a transitive action on the part of the reader (a deeply moral action), in which he sets his eyes and mind to follow what the evangelists, their secretaries, and editors have put before him. ("It seemed good to me . . . , having followed all things closely for some time past, to write an orderly account for you, most excellent Theophilus, that you may know the truth concerning [these] things . . ." [RSV]) But, in the second place, such reading also involves the reader's action of putting himself into the narrative and of seeing himself as one whom these very events befall, of seeing himself as the evangelists might have seen him, had he been among those acting out this narrative. Hence, such reading is a translation, a translation of the reader into the narrative.

Third, it is also a translation of the matter and personas of the narrative into the reader's own imaginative representation of the present. And since these narratives and pericopes have a specific character, this translation must have a corresponding character. It must be a taking up of Jesus as the evangelists present him, integumented in and by the binary of suffering and power, and placing him as such in the reader's imagination; so that from the reader's imagination arises the query: "Am I not also so integumented?" For a translation, viz., reading, of Jesus stripped of that binary in which the Gospels represent him would be a work of fancy and not of reading. Such a Jesus would be a silhouette, not an actor-patient who moves and intensifies the imagination. He would be a figure torn out of his world, out of the circumpressing action that gave him definition. Apart from this binary of suffering and power the Jesus who is to be translated could not become the focal interest of men who are interested in human faithfulness because they are already situated in a field that exacts faith of some kind from them. And therefore apart from the binary he could not be a new beginner and beginning of such faith. But when, in the transaction between reader and narrative, Jesus does enter the imagination, he enters as an enworlded man, as a man whose world is God-Ruling, as a man in the God that Paul described to the Athenians as "him in whom we live and move and have our being."

Finally, one more transaction takes place in such reflexive reading—or *may* take place, for, as we shall state more fully below, it is not a transaction that intent reading alone can effect. This last transaction is the transformation of the entire reality of which reader, narrative subject matter, and the relation between them are parts. Such a transformation is not wrought—by translation or by any other effort. It is rather an overcoming of the reader, an awakening, in which the messenger of the new age, the age itself appearing in his conduct, and the reader as the man awakening in response to that conduct, all draw together and coalesce in an encompassing and newly perceived totality. Such an awakening is not a response to this or that—to the transposition of the reader into Jesus' age or of Jesus into his. It is, to be sure, an awakening to the messenger, but to him as an actor or persona in whom his environing age forcibly appears and speaks as the reader's own. It is also an awakening to the reader's own world, but to that world as a new or forgotten world of which Christ is a true effect, a "first born," a "pioneer." It is an awakening of the kind characterized by the writers of the Gospels as a being "born again" and described by each of them in a particular idiom.

When, for example—as the Gospel of John describes such things —men pass from darkness into light, they come upon their world and their own existence in it as vessels of light and reason. And the relief in which Jesus stands in their perception, the primacy he occupies in their field of view, is the effect of his conduct, attitude, and speech as the very image and personification of light dispelling darkness and of generosity driving out private love. Jesus becomes the center of men's consciousness of conflict between the power of darkness and the power of light. In this kind of awakening, he is Light streaming from Light and repairing the damaged eye; he is Life flowing from Life and quickening the visible field; he is Logos with God from the beginning giving beauty to all being. And God is, correspondingly, the Power that affects men in all these ways through this man who is a human image of the universal action of Light giving light, of Truth drawing understanding to itself, and of Unity composing the ever-changing field of life. One affection pervades the entire view of self, of other, and of the age in such awakening: the affection of loving reason or intellectual love overspreading the darkness.

This same living connectedness of the elements of faith is evident in the other modes in which a new world arises and becomes the horizon and the arena of men's existence. When they awaken to their world and to their own existence as beings who are being liberated from groaning in the slavery of lethargy and the rule of the law of habitual selfishness, they do so perceiving Jesus Christ as the embodiment of liberty. But he, in turn, as a liberator proffering a painful escape from these self-forged chains, belongs to a far wider world of free and creative action. Correspondingly, for men who come upon new life in this encounter and liberation, God is principally the Summoner from habit to transcendental freedom. But more than that, he is the moral beauty lying beyond all known patterns, codes, and laws, empowering men to venture into the unknown with the pioneer of faith. And one affection pervades the whole polarity of self and field of assailing and persuasive power. It is courageousness, a self-denying courage—and an invincible sense of being destined to share in the shaping and reshaping action of God-Ruling.

What is true of these ways of awakening holds also for the way of faith that we have described throughout these pages. This third way does not obviate the former but accompanies them and widens them with a fuller and more enduring meaning. It is the way of awakening in which men come to consciousness of themselves, of their fellow beings, and of their shared world as integers belonging to a surmounting whole. In such awakening, Christ appears as the inventor and new beginning of a way of human faithfulness. He suffers diminution and enlargement equally, as the good-pleasure of God-Ruling. He is the definite exemplar, the concrete appearance, the visible beauty of the government under which all beings arrive, flourish, and depart. And God, again in corresponding fashion, is the Rule that brings Jesus to his special configuration as a man, that sets him in the earth like a new Adam, and that draws all other men into the field of his good—pleasure in a comparable fashion. The God so apprehended in this awakening is not exclusive of the gods who dawn upon man reasoning or man willing and deciding in faithfulness. He is still Truth, but as Truth he is more than the ineffable Idea which satisfies the appetite of reason; he is regulating Idea, the Idea whose essence is govering power in the mind. And as the summoning Word calling men to singlehearted obedience, he is more than a transcendental sense of duty in men's practical reason; he is a coercive God, burning in the prophet's bones until the prophet consents to play his part.

A double affection overtakes the man awakened to this Christ and God, emanating from the figure of Jesus and from the world of divine ruling and fixing itself in his consciousness: the twofold affection of shipwreck and of gladness bound together in amazement. In rudimentary form, this double affection qualifies every life. In Jesus of Nazareth it becomes the form of his being. When in the act of reading or of hearing or of reflecting the radial man of this radial world collides with the actor of the Gospels and recognizes his own bondage to him through the sharing of these common affections, the way is open to him to perceive his own life also as a moment in the age of God.

The Gospels represent Jesus as a God-shaped man, as a locus in which the ruling action of God appears. It appears in him as Jesus acquires friends and disciples and takes the leadership of a new movement in human history—in a word, as Jesus grows large; and it also appears as Jesus loses his friends and disciples, sees his cause meeting defeat, and finds himself taken prisoner and condemned—in a word, as Jesus grows small. No reading or even close study of these books can propose seriously that this Messiah or Rabbi or friend of Simon the son of Jonas did not think of himself as God-shaped. The thoughts that passed through his mind may not be ours to share. But the actions and words the reader learns about refer to God, and since actions and words belong to conduct and conduct makes up what we mean by the word person, we may accept this God-shapedness as constituent of Jesus persona. Indeed, we may take Jesus' actions and words together as a persona of God-Ruling, a mask of the *basileia tou theou*, for God-Ruling was the burden of his part in life. Hence, whatever the reader makes of this representation of Jesus, whether he judge the picture to be one of a numinous and unapproachable theophany or of a friend to all kinds of men, to be a picture of an incarnation of a different order of being or of the utmost evolutionary outcome of the race, this one element remains constant. As a figure who attracts or fends men off, Jesus' relation to God is part and parcel of his effect on others. He befriends and alienates other men as a man who refers himself to God and so refers the interpreter also to the God dominating and shaping his persona. No demythologizing or modernization of Jesus can blink that fact.[8]

8. It seems to me that Professor Paul van Buren, in his book *The Secular Meaning of the Gospel*, New York (1963), overlooks this elementary fact. The being that theologians describe as God may well be unacceptable to the minds of many today, but God did not mean loving human conduct as Jesus used that word. God meant the prevenient maker of human suffering, repentance, and gladness.

The event in which this perception breaks is comparable, no doubt, to a "birth" of faith, though human faith lends itself better to description as rebirth than it does to interpretation as birth, since faith of some kind or other has always been coming to be in the binary of suffering and power. But no studiedly self-conscious reading of the Gospels, however well grounded it be, can bring about such a transformation of the biblical Jesus and the reader's awareness of himself. The collision, the discovery on the reader's part that he shares with this representative man a common embodiment in a field of energy and of patterns of action he did not choose, the realization that he dies and rises in ways that can be compared to Christ's diminutions and enlargements—none of these things takes place according to the rules of exegesis or meditation or whatever practice may be learned. These collisions seem instead to be accidents, events that originate outside the scope or reach of men's attention and befall them unprepared.

Such an accident befell readers in one part of Christendom little more than a half century ago, when men were reading the New Testament in the heavy awareness then recently created by historical research that Jesus of Nazareth belongs to an alien culture, exhibits an alien mind, acts out of a strange sense of time and an apocalyptic hope, and inhabits a world that can never again be naïvely identified with the reader's world.[9] Whoever acquaints himself with the development and the details of this research into the "historical Jesus" will appreciate the great momentum it gathered and its crushing effects on Bible-centered piety. In contrast, however, to the systematic and methodical ways in which men make their historical inquiries, the processes of history in the making—the determinations of men's actions by actions of the "great world of action"—are marked and twisted by accidents, with the result that hard-earned convictions and conclusions become obsolete. Such a befalling overturned the conviction of that age about the infinite remoteness of Jesus. For it

9. The great history of this research is Albert Schweitzer's *The Quest of the Historical Jesus*, first published in 1906 (trans. W. Montgomery, New York [1950]).

was an accident so far as biblical research is concerned that men living in the days before 1914 shortly came to know what life is like in the face of an imminent and cataclysmic end of human affairs. Yet that accident and the bursts of violence succeeding it across the earth have opened to the interested reader fissures for perception of the world of Jesus, amplified to audibility again something of the authority weighting his cry in the ears of his hearers, and aroused again something of the fear, astonishment, and amazed horror with which men greeted him. Total and global conflict, as political fact without and as evil demon within, have thinned and fenestrated the great barrier of remoteness walling the world of the prophet whose words and being were filled with the Kingdom of God, so that here and there again he is visible and his conduct intelligible in the reader's world. Therefore, although scholars and others are powerless to make Jesus of Nazareth a modern man fitting into their own generation, other powers do "modernize" Jesus willy-nilly, thrusting these worlds together in the focus of a single vision.

In such circumstances, when men undergo affections that they perceive also and preeminently in another affected man, the time is ripe for them to see freshly, to see his faith-conduct within a newly defined perimeter of the field of existence, to discern more sharply the springs of his believing, and to share in the moral action of such believing as the circumpressing field of power calls out of pioneers in the unexplored territory of God-Ruling. Then men are readier to confer a captaincy for their own suffering on someone who has gone before them in experiencing the hitherto unseen, unheard, and unnoticed. They are readier to believe, not as men commanded to assent but as men constrained to hold dear the evidences of generosity, of beauty, of stringency, and of steadfastness that appear in the age befalling them.

Faith struggles for form and fitness at such time-points of intersection, when one world befalls another, as the world of God-Ruling in the time-point of Jesus of Nazareth befell the Roman centurion, the Samarian woman at the well, Saul of Tarsus, and other twice-born men and women. When men admire

Jesus, as they often do, despite their indifference to church creeds and to theological ascriptions to him of special metaphysical properties, they admire him for his way toward others, toward the neighbor or near one, and also for his carelessness toward himself. They admire him as a man both full of care and careless. Jesus acts on such admirers as an attractively generous being, inviting others to share in his own conduct and to share in a corresponding world that, although it presses hard on men and strikes them down, makes them glad; despair cannot contain it. Such gladly astonished men feel themselves being moved not only to follow Jesus in his way but to act in a larger and finer system of action than they had recognized before, unconstricted by distinctions of person, of caste, of origin, or of social function. And when, conversely, they are constrained by Jesus' ungreediness for life and by his recklessness of self to duplicate his conduct in their own lives, they feel themselves summoned not by Jesus alone but by an exigent and austere sublimity appearing in and about him.

Such attraction may work slowly and steadily, or briefly, intermittently, and weakly. But when it acts and as it acts, men fall within an authority that is more than Jesus' charisma. It is the authorizing power that augments Jesus. Consequently, however this action of Jesus on witnesses and readers be interpreted, whether as the sharing of manliness and courage by one who typifies human strength in its finest proportions or as the liberating of fear-weakened people from dehumanizing bondage by a redeemer descended from heaven, Jesus does not act out of resources that are his alone but by the power that is shaping him. Accordingly, he affects others by his conduct. His conduct, in turn, is his government of himself within the action of the world opposing him and informing him. His self-government is his conviction-in-motion that his own life is a theater of that action and that the pattern of that action "desires," "needs," "requires," "commands" him to become the place of its livelier and richer manifestation. His conviction is that his being is a new locus of God-Ruling. Faith, perception, action, and existence are thus all one thing in him: the rule of self within the ruling action that appears everywhere. That is the faith and conduct that men admire when their admiration is of Jesus of Nazareth.

When Jesus so appeals to men, he does so as a God-shaped person. Without God he vanishes as a concrete personality. Two aspects of his persona, as the Gospels present him, exhibit this shaping action in him. First of all, there is his awareness—expressed in parable and epigram—that the world in which he moves is the ruling conduct of God. And second, there is his consciousness—expressed in counseling with his disciples about his course of action—that the intentions which inwardly determine his conduct are intended by God. Outwardly that which is objective to him is God-Ruling and inwardly that which is objective to him is God-Intending. Hence, he moves and acts in the action of the Kingdom, and the Kingdom moves and acts in the action of Jesus. The consequence that these two faces of Jesus' conduct make plain to the reader is one with which we are now familiar. Whoever wishes to explore Jesus' humanity to understand the example of his conduct, to comprehend his stature as a pioneer of faithfulness, must begin by exploring Jesus' world, which is God-Ruling. But whoever would explore Jesus' world can enter it only by beginning where his own world intersects it, at the points where it diminishes and enlarges him, giving him opportunity to recognize the unattended geneses of human faithfulness in himself. For radial man, therefore, the interpretation of Jesus begins as an interpretation of the same encompassing reality under two aspects and two names: the ruling action of which Jesus is the voice and the "finger" and the enworlding field of action that presses the interpreter.

The parables Jesus told about the Kingdom of God point to some of these intersections. As parts of Jesus' verbal conduct—which in turn belongs to his faith-conduct as a whole within his world of God-Ruling—they signify Jesus' interestedness in that world. But while doing so they also refer the reader to his own daily world, and so they indicate the "grounds" on which Jesus chose to meet other men, the actions within which he sought to enliven their perception by sharing with them his own. The phenomena of seed changing into living and growing grain; rain falling on the farmland of the honest and the devious alike; the futility of insuring for the next day and the gladness of being free of care of self; the vineyard owner's giving of equal payment for unequal hours of work; the dinner party that men attend through coercion; the woman's finding of her lost money and her rejoicing over recovery of it; the father's gladness in his reunion with his estranged son—all of these parables as well as the many others suggest to the reader the kind of action in the ruling of God that Jesus perceived as typical action. And when the reader sets the parables in the context of the whole of Jesus' conduct within the action of God-Ruling him, they grow more vivid and eloquent, just as Jesus' actions of healing, forgiving sin, and dying for his cause become more parabolic when they are recognized as belonging to his perceptions of God-Ruling.

Present-day readers are often aware—some acutely aware— that each of these parables (in each of its several editorial versions) had its own special occasion for assuming significance in the lives of the early Christians, and that therefore each and all of them reflect the cares of the first churches superimposed on the perceptions and language of Jesus. Nevertheless, they, like Jesus' other conduct, exhibit certain features that we may take to be features of Jesus' perception of God-Ruling.

All of the parables mentioned above, for example, despite their various particular histories of development, indicate a divine action that is unfettered or—to use a word that is more adequate in its strictest meaning—absolute.[10] They indicate an action that is strong and free of restraints. The rejoicing of the woman over the finding of the lost coin suggests the thirst of life that belongs to poverty. The story of the vineyard owner reflects the pride of liberality that accompanies dominion. The parable of the anemones in their bright colors embodies acquaintance with the lavishness of providence or good luck. The rain that falls on just

10. *Absolvere*: to set free, of chains, fetters, etc. See Skeat, *Etymological Dictionary of the English Language*.

and unjust demonstrates the merciful indifference of nature toward human distinctions. The parable of the host recruiting unwilling guests from the alleys recalls the impatience of those who have not only a good will but the means to execute it.

In these ways Jesus' parables also humanize the environment by making each event in it understandable on a homely scale. He imputes many intentions to God-Ruling that are similar to human intentions and dispositions. But at the same time these parables of the homely and the common take up ordinary passions and everyday engagements of men and set them in the sphere of ultimate power and authority, of final beauty and holiness, so that they become times and places of glory. Therefore, individually and collectively, these and the other parables, epigrams, and words of Jesus dramatize no one face of God-Ruling so much as his free, independent, unrestrained good-pleasure. And as such dramatizations and demonstrations they become parables not only of Jesus' great world of action but also of Jesus' life itself, where homeliness and glory merge and diminution and enlargement meet on a new scale of faithfulness.

Yet the good-pleasure that appears here is not complete or self-contained. It takes trouble. It broadens itself to include the lost, the unjust, the uninvited, the latecomer, the improvident, and the weak as well as the strong. In the language of an older and perhaps a more familiar piety, we should have called this pervading quality of the actions in the parables the quality of mercy, but possibly for us today a better word is generosity. The action of God-Ruling is generous action, widening action, generating action. But it is a stringent generosity that leaves those men who do not swiftly greet it emptier than they had been before. It also upsets conventions of the age and brings judgment on those who, although they see and hear the forces of love, suffering, agony, and desire in men and in the happenings of nature, do not recognize themselves as members of the binary of power and suffering from which God-Ruling and human faithfulness emerge.

The thrust of Jesus' conduct, therefore, is the showing of the Kingdom of God widening itself. Quite obivously, this conduct is no argumentation. It is only a demonstration, a method of showing. No *via negativa* or *via eminentia* could prevail here. For God-Ruling is neither like nor wholly unlike the age as men customarily live in it, and therefore no chains of inference lead the mind to a surmise of his nature. The burden of Jesus' conduct is to disclose the world opposing and informing him as a theater of action. The motive of that action is the divine good-pleasure. The quality of that action is generosity. The mass of that action is power. The appearance of that action is Jesus' own persona. The goal of that action is human faithfulness wrought out of the experience of diminishment and enlargement in which that great action may appear again in glory. God-Ruling is a powerful, generous, and swift good-pleasure intersecting the human world at every point, now making men small, now making them great, but never letting them be.

Afterword

Whoever thinks of man and man's faith as such awakening will also have to think of God as near and not as removed from us by infinite qualitative difference or by a metaphysical abyss. If we take our departure from the correlation of suffering and power then the power to which we give the name of king or rule of our lives will be a power we recognize as lying in our ambience and as indeed being the very matter and agency of our world. Such a way of thinking about God may seem to have little resemblance to the idea of God that earlier theology has handed down, but the differences between the langauge of other times and our own may in fact be much greater than the differences between the intentions and experiences conveyed in them. In any case, we have at least to recall that the more traditional theological concepts of God formed in a culture that associated deity with changelessness, with self-sufficiency, and often even with aloofness. They formed in a culture that spent much of its religious energy seeking a divine medicine against time, passion, and decay. That world has gone. Our experience is of another world of movement and power. We should not, however, confuse the reality of

God with the categories that men prefer when they speak of perfection and of deity. We should, rather, cling to the reality all men know through their suffering and through their faith as faith emerges in their affections, their believing, and their actions.

To be sure, the work of clarifying our experience and ordering our thoughts in a way suitable to a wider consciousness of our affective being and of our world as the theater of God-Ruling will take a long time. And no doubt this way of thinking will raise more questions than it appears to settle. But human faith is not so much a sum of answers as it is a way of seeing and acting, and books about faith have first of all to describe what faithful men see and believe to be real. Description has been my chief aim in these pages. My intention has not been to dismiss older ways of thinking but to begin to take our older ways and still older issues of religion and faith and God and place them in the light that is thrown in our own perceptions of the new man today who has his being in a world of power that is forever disquieting him and reshaping him. Is it not possible that this man, whom we all know well, is experiencing the terrible joy of being made and made again by a ruling power that he knows but does not know that he knows? Is it not possible that in his daily despair and occasional gladness he can accept these moments of awakening, in a world where Jesus of Nazareth has gone before, as telling him what God is? God is our determination and our freedom, our living and our dying.

"Our mouth is open to you, Corinthians" Paul wrote to his busy and disputatious parishioners; "our heart is wide. You are not restricted by us, but you are restricted in your own affections. In return . . . widen [yourselves] also."[11]

11. II Cor. 6:11-13 (RSV).

Index

72 73 74 75 10 9 8 7 6 5 4 3 2 1